BODY LANGUAGE IN RELATIONSHIPS

Overcoming Common Problems Series

For a full list of titles please contact
Sheldon Press, Marylebone Road, London NW1 4DU

Beating the Blues
SUSAN TANNER AND JILLIAN BALL

Birth Over Thirty
SHEILA KITZINGER

Body Language
How to read others' thoughts by their
gestures
ALLAN PEASE

Calm Down
How to cope with frustration and anger
DR PAUL HAUCK

Changing Course
How to take charge of your career
SUE DYSON AND STEPHEN HOARE

Comfort for Depression
JANET HORWOOD

Complete Public Speaker
GYLES BRANDRETH

Coping Successfully with Migraine
SUE DYSON

**Coping Successfully with Your
Child's Asthma**
DR PAUL CARSON

**Coping Successfully with Your
Hyperactive Child**
DR PAUL CARSON

**Coping Successfully with Your
Irritable Bowel**
ROSEMARY NICOL

**Coping Successfully with Your
Second Child**
FIONA MARSHALL

Coping with Anxiety and Depression
SHIRLEY TRICKETT

Coping with Blushing
DR ROBERT EDELMANN

Coping with Cot Death
SARAH MURPHY

Coping with Depression and Elation
DR PATRICK McKEON

Coping with Stress
A Woman's Guide
DR GEORGIA WITKIN-LANOIL

Coping with Strokes
DR TOM SMITH

Coping with Suicide
DR DONALD SCOTT

Coping with Thrush
CAROLINE CLAYTON

**Curing Arthritis –
The Drug-Free Way**
MARGARET HILLS

Curing Arthritis Diet Book
MARGARET HILLS

**Curing Coughs, Colds and Flu –
The Drug-Free Way**
MARGARET HILLS

Curing Illness – The Drug-Free Way
MARGARET HILLS

Depression
DR PAUL HAUCK

Divorce and Separation
ANGELA WILLANS

Don't Blame Me!
How to stop blaming yourself
and other people
TONY GOUGH

**Everything You Need to Know
about Adoption**
MAGGIE JONES

**Everything You Need to Know
about Osteoporosis**
ROSEMARY NICOL

**Everything You Need to Know
about Shingles**
DR ROBERT YOUNGSON

**Family First Aid and Emergency
Handbook**
DR ANDREW STANWAY

Feverfew
DR STEWART JOHNSON

Fight Your Phobia and Win
DAVID LEWIS

Getting Along with People
DIANNE DOUBTFIRE

Getting Married
JOANNA MOORHEAD

Goodbye Backache
DR DAVID IMRIE WITH
COLLEEN DIMSON

BODY LANGUAGE
IN RELATIONSHIPS

David Cohen

SHELDON PRESS

LONDON

First published in Great Britain 1992
Sheldon Press, SPCK, Marylebone Road, London NW1 4DU

Illustrations by Peter Cox

British Library Cataloguing-in-Publication Data

A catalogue record for this book is available
from the British Library

ISBN 0-85969-655-3

Typeset by Pioneer Associates, Perthshire
Printed in Great Britain by
Mackays of Chatham plc, Chatham, Kent

Contents

Introduction

Knowing what body language means gives you the chance to see what someone else is really feeling, even when they don't want to tell you.

Most of the photographs in the book were taken during the making of a film which I directed called *The Pleasure Principle*, a comedy about a confused modern man (played by Peter Firth) and his relationships with four very different women (played by Haydn Gwynne, Lynsey Baxter, Lysette Anthony and Sara Mair Thomas). The pictures were taken by Chris Schwartz during breaks in the filming and during rehearsals. Although I did not set out to make a film about body language, there were many expressive examples of body language at work to be found on the set as we rehearsed and shot.

Two of the photographs come from another film on mid-life crises made by a friend of mine, Lindsay Knight. I'm grateful to her for permission to use them.

David Cohen
August 1992

1

Can You See How I Feel?

Sally and Mark are on their first date. They are sitting in a wine bar. Sally likes Mark very much but she doesn't want to let on. Mark likes Sally too but he hates it when women act so cool. It makes him nervous. Sally doesn't realise how nervous she's making him.

Mark's right hand is playing with his wine glass. His left hand is on his knee, patting himself. When he smiles at Sally, his smile often tails off abruptly.

Mark would love to stop fidgeting and take Sally's hand. At one point, he edges his hand closer, then moves it away, then brings it closer to her. Sally's hand stays put a little too far away for him to take it easily.

Both of them know something isn't right but they don't know *what* isn't right.

If Sally could see under the table she would see further signs of nervousness. Mark's ankles are off the floor and they are locked together. If Sally

Figure 1 *The wine bar. Mark and Sally.*

1

could read body language she would know three things:

1. Mark really does like her.
2. He is nervous, because he doesn't know how *she* feels.
3. He lacks confidence and is caught in the approach-avoidance trap.

Many of us don't know how to read body language well. No one ever teaches us how to do it. You pick up knowledge as you go along. Almost inevitably, that means you see less than you could about how the people around you feel and, indeed, about how you yourself feel.

Hidden feelings

'Body language' is a phrase that has slipped into our language over the last twenty years. It reflects the way we have become more interested in thinking psychologically. We want to understand ourselves and other people and we look for accurate ways of doing so. One reason why body language is interesting is that it gives us insight into the hidden thoughts, feelings and anxieties of others – and into our own wishes and fears.

Sigmund Freud, the founder of psychoanalysis, has had a profound effect on how we talk about how we behave.

Take these phrases:

Jeremy has an 'inferiority complex'.
Sarah is 'repressed' about men.
Jonesy has 'too much ego'.

Psychoanalysis suggests we have many unconscious desires. We repress wishes. Often we don't know the real motives for our actions. Freud, who had a playful side to him, enjoyed dissecting jokes, mistakes and slips of the tongue. These 'para-

praxes', as he called them, allowed the unconscious to burst through. The unconscious is primitive, teeming with forbidden desires that are kept in check by society.

Freud analysed what his patients said and remembered. They lay on his famous couch – now in the Freud Museum in London – and talked. Freud didn't often observe people's behaviour in real life but he saw the importance of body language. One patient, Freud wrote in 1905, might be lying as he spoke, but he betrayed himself through his fingertips: 'they chattered away nervously'.

Our fingers, arms, legs, ankles do 'chatter away' and reveal a great deal about our hopes, our fears, our anxieties and our personalities. Our gestures, large and small, say a great deal – especially perhaps when it comes to love and sex. Most of us can very easily become neurotic about whether or not we are loved and desired. These neuroses often sneak out in our body language.

To understand body language you have to learn to observe other people – and yourself – accurately. Throughout this book, I'm going to offer examples and case histories which I hope will make some complicated ideas clear and will also help you understand the non-verbal communication going on around you all the time. Sometimes, someone doesn't have to say a word to tell you what they feel.

How body language works

In the wine bar, Mark has decided to be bold. He leans forward and puts his hand a mere two inches from Sally's (see figures 2 and 3).

Mark's sense of timing is not good. Just as he puts his hand down closer to Sally, a rather attractive man walks across to another table in

Figure 2 *Two hands close together. Both have palms down. His hand is extended towards her. Hers remains close but closed.*

Figure 3 *Two hands close together. One palm down, the other palm half up. This is clearly an invitation to take the hand.*

the bar. A few seconds later, Sally tosses her hair back (see figure 4). She looks to the side and gobbles two mouthfuls of peanuts.

There is a psychologist in the bar. Like all conscientious psychologists, he's equipped with a stopwatch. He notices that Sally now nibbles her peanuts quicker than before. Then she takes two quick sips of wine from her glass. Then she brushes her hand across her mouth (see figure 5).

All of Sally's movements are small and perfectly normal, yet they reveal a lot about what she is feeling.

Figure 4 *Sally tossing head*

Figure 5 *Sally brushing lips*

4

Children learn a few things about body language in the course of growing up. By the age of ten, they know that if they're lying and they don't want to give the game away, they should try not to look down or clap their hands over their mouth. We all have some insights into body language, unless we are emotionally blind. You don't need a degree in psychology to know that the woman holding her head in her hand in figure 6 is not having a good time.

The woman in the picture is sending a very clear message: I am miserable. Our messages are generally more subtle, however. Often, I don't want to give away what I feel. Do I really want you to know that I am having a bad time at work, that I am worried about money or that I'm afraid my lover finds me less attractive? No. So I tough it out. We have lunch. I don't mope. To the unperceptive eye, I seem O.K. Only the acute observer will pick up small, but important, clues that reveal my inner feelings.

The more intimate the situation, the more of our 'real selves' we lay on the line, the more our body language may reveal – often against our will. Sometimes, our body will tell us truths we don't know – and aren't ready for.

Figure 6 *The distance here between the man and the woman is considerable. She is looking down, turned away from him.*

'Body language' sounds like a contradiction. After all, we speak with our *mouths*. But, increasingly, research shows it *is* a language. You can think of it in terms of words and sentences, which are built up of intentional gestures and unconscious 'signals' one is not aware of. Some of these are fleeting, fluttering movements – micro-signals – like Sally brushing her hand across her mouth, which can only be caught through concentrated observation. A single gesture, like shaking someone's hand, is a 'word'. A series of interrelated gestures, known as a cluster, is a 'sentence'.

Look at figure 7. This picture shows a cluster of positive gestures. The man leans forward. His eyes look straight at the woman. His hand is moving towards her. There is nothing subtle or secret in the sentence he is saying: 'I like you, and I want to be close to you'.

Body language can reinforce or contradict what we are saying. If you are having to be polite to someone you don't like, you may spout all the right words, but your body may rebel. You may shake their hand for as short a time as possible, or try to avoid eye contact. Here, body language contradicts spoken language. You are sending

Figure 7 *The man is showing a cluster of positive gestures.*

two different signals. The verbal one says 'I like you'; the non-verbal one says 'I don't like you'. If the receiver understands body language, he won't be fooled.

Unless, that is, you are a superb manipulator of body language and know just how to make it look *as if* you really feel positive. Only a body language expert could spot the tiny giveaway clues that reveal your real feelings.

Animal behaviour

When the attractive man came into the wine bar, Sally ate more quickly, fidgeted with her glass, then brushed her hand across her mouth. Sally was not particularly conscious of fancying the man yet; apart from all these actions, she also changed the position of her hand relative to Mark's. She didn't withdraw it but turned it up so that her palm was now in a less submissive position to his hand. Brushing her hand across her mouth and tossing her head are *displacement activities*. For centuries, human beings have engaged in displacement activities without knowing it. We know about them now mainly because of studies of birds like herring gulls and avocets.

Ethology is the study of animal behaviour in the wild. When ethologists in the 1950s observed herring gulls, they noticed something unusual. A herring gull who wanted to mate but couldn't, because available females were more impressed by larger gulls, often acted in what seemed to be a very strange way. The frustrated gull would run back and forth to the limit of its territory. It would move restlessly and would often start pecking frantically at the ground. The gull might also behave like that if he could not fight with another male who was coming close to his territory.

Ethologists like the Nobel prizewinner Niko Tinbergen claimed the herring gull was releasing as much of his pent-up sexual or aggressive energy as possible. The frantic movements didn't achieve the goal the bird wanted – mating or fighting – but at least they discharged some of his physiological tension.

We may not be flattered to find our behaviour compared to a bird's. Yet the herring gull has something to teach us. When Sally brushed her hand against her mouth and tossed her head it was a rather subtler release of sexual tension than frantic pecking. Sally didn't know what she was doing any more than the herring gull did, but you can learn to observe such micro-gestures.

When things go wrong

Sex is one of the most powerful of biological drives. Surveys show that 94 per cent of men and 86 per cent of women have sexual fantasies. Only the need to eat, to sleep and to drink are stronger biological drives.

Social needs, however, conflict with biology. As Freud observed, civilization would be impossible if everyone allowed their libido free rein. In every society, sexual behaviour is controlled. You can't go up to perfect strangers in the street and tell them that you desire them madly. Individuals who do that are dangerous and out of control.

Yet ordinary, well-controlled people do lead rich fantasy lives in which they engage in all kinds of sexual behaviour. All this creates tension – and tension which often expresses itself unwittingly in our body language. Desire sometimes can be very embarrassing.

Most of us are familiar with being nervous at a party because there is someone there you want to impress. You manage quite skilfully to join the group they are in (see figure 8).

Figure 8 *The dynamics of this group are interesting. Both men are vying for supremacy in different ways. Note the position of the heads and shoulders. All faces are turned towards the man who has a 'wise' look with his finger on his chin – a typical 'I am appraising you' pose. But the other man has put himself higher – a classic way of trying to achieve dominance.*

But now things start to go wrong. You start to feel a little over-excited because you are so near the person you want to impress. You find you can't think of anything to say. You start to blush. You can feel yourself staring too much. You start to sweat.

The worst is yet to come. You start fidgeting with your glass and spill some wine over your shirt.

One man I knew in such a predicament became sure that if only he ate something, he would know what to say. He grabbed a cocktail stick with pineapple and cheese on it. Still a bag of nerves, he promptly dropped it all over the woman he wanted to chat up. He went beetroot. Needless to say, a relationship did not develop.

These kinds of mishaps don't just happen to the socially inept. A friend went out with a glamorous woman. She made fun of him when he got jealous. He didn't know whether or not she was also seeing other men. He didn't dare confront her. He became very clumsy. He often spilled cups of coffee and glasses of wine. When he was driving with her, he often crashed gears and couldn't shift them properly. Once he tripped over her dog. His lack of co-ordination betrayed his fear and frustration.

In relationships, there are great advantages to understanding your own and your partner's body language. It allows you to have a sense of what is really going on before too many words are spoken. You can tell if you want someone and whether someone wants you. And, less happily, you can tell when things are going wrong.

A brief history of body language

Great writers like Shakespeare have known for centuries that posture and gesture reflect mood. In *Twelfth Night*, Olivia's steward Malvolio makes himself ridiculous by wearing yellow garters and behaving strangely. But there were no systematic studies of body language till the 1960s. Then the American psychologist Paul Ekman examined how good we were at reading non-verbal messages off people's faces. An English psychologist, Michael Argyle at the University of Oxford, studied other kinds of body language – gestures, how close we come to someone, if we touch people and where we do. Argyle and Ekman both stressed that body language was really a *language*. You couldn't look at one gesture in isolation. You had to examine the complete pattern of gestures, postures and tones of voice to understand the whole of a situation. Part of the art of reading body language is putting all the clues about 'clusters' together.

Interaction

Argyle and his co-workers claimed that when people met, talked or did anything together, this snippet of behaviour should be seen as an 'interaction'. It sounds like jargon but it does emphasise how many different factors are at play between people. A good way to examine any interaction is to analyse three elements of it – its context, its text and its subtext.

The *context* is the general situation in which a meeting or an exchange between people occurs.

Going to lunch is a different kind of event depending on whom you go to lunch with. A quick bite with a colleague from the office, lunch with a lover or lunch with someone whom you might go out with will all have different dynamics.

Next time you're in a restaurant, try using your knowledge of body language to guess what kind of lunch the couple at the next table are having. Look at the distance between them, for example. Perhaps one of them has a note-book or other 'work tool' on the table to emphasise that they see it as professional. But are they poised to move closer?

The *text* is the actual words spoken in any encounter. Words aren't everything. If you were just given a transcript of what was said in any interaction, it wouldn't begin to give you the full sense of what was going on. Imagine a couple having lunch, for example. The 2-line transcript of their conversation that you get might run:

WOMAN : I love you.
MAN : Do you really?

You can't tell from the transcript whether 'I love you' was a sudden declaration of passion, a cosy but not surprising truth, or a gibe because the woman was angry. Identical words: different meanings.

The *subtext* consists of the intonations and the body language used. These should convey similar kinds of information about the warmth and closeness of the encounter. People do not only rely on words to form an impression of an interaction. The tone of voice and non-verbal cues amount to over half the evidence on which they base their judgment of any situation. If these non-verbal cues contradict what is being said, people worry and think they may be being deceived.

Does she still care?

Often, body language provides clues we would rather not have.

Let us imagine another couple at lunch. Jane and John do not sound relaxed. John has taken Jane's hand. He seems to be trying to placate her. Yet he knows she hates such public displays of affection. And *she* knows he knows she hates it. It was after his attempt to take her hand that she snapped: 'I love you'. The phrase is often now used ironically, when someone is being irritating.

The context and text of any interaction are usually easy to describe. The subtext can be more ambiguous and often involves convoluted feelings of the kind: *he knows she hates this so why is she doing it?* Tiny moves, complex feelings. And no one says a word.

It's because of such convolutions that insight into body language is so fascinating.

Masks

Body language also pierces our masks.

Human beings learn to wear masks early – and many of us do it very well. Many of the non-verbal clues to feelings are subtle and fleeting. To read them is a little like deciphering the pattern on a scarf of someone who walks by. You can do it, but it takes skill and practice.

What gets through the mask are what psychologists call 'leaky cues' – cues that we don't mean to give but can't control. It's quite easy to control facial expressions. If you don't want to look sad, you can fake it. It's much harder to control our tone of voice or our gestures. These 'leak'. Study them and you will soon know much of what others are thinking.

The way individuals speak reflects their personality. Some people boom and talk endlessly; others

are hard to draw out; some people are clipped. In this book I argue that people with particular kinds of personality are likely to have a particular kind of body style which will clash with other people's. Some of the best-founded personality research contrasts *extraverts*, who are outgoing, social, quick, inaccurate, love jokes, impatient and have a quick metabolism, with *introverts*, who are accurate, worry far more, are slower to arouse and far less social-skilled. One kind of personality isn't better than another. Each is a style, but it's a style that comes through in body language.

In relationships, many people feel under pressure not to show what they are feeling. We are living through a period of complex social changes which makes many of us feel safer behind our masks.

Changing attitudes

In *The Godfather*, Al Pacino flees New York for Sicily after he has committed a murder to save his family. He falls in love with a girl in the village where he is staying. He begins to woo her in the time-honoured way. He calls on her father and asks for permission to walk out with his daughter. Man and woman walk together under the wary eye of chaperones. There is no question of a kiss or any physical contact between them till they are married.

Everything now is more muddled. We have a bewildering variety of relationships – marriage, live-in lovers, casual affairs, affairs with an ex-spouse. One marriage in three ends in divorce. Thirty-seven per cent of children are born in one-parent families. No one is sure what is morally and socially acceptable. Once divorce was a disgrace. People only lived together if they were married. Those who 'lived in sin' would never be invited to a respectable dinner party. Now there would be few dinner parties if you excluded divorcees and those who live together outside marriage.

Gender bending

The roles of men and women have changed. Men used to be regarded as simple creatures. Now they can apparently choose to be macho men, 'new men', 'new lads', or, in America at least, deeply sensitive 'critturs' who are trying to get in touch with their wild hairy selves. Feminism has made many women far more assertive. They are more likely to take the initiative in relationships.

Our body posture, our gestures, and the way we dress reflects the modern profusion and confusion of roles (see figures 9, 10, 11).

These changes haven't made relationships easier. Partners now feel under pressure to be interesting, supportive, good in bed, good with the children, successful at work. There are many roles to play and fewer rules to play by.

Pundits keep on saying that you must get the most out of your life – and an important part of that is one's love life. Being frustrated, and not getting the most out of one's experiences, now rank as the ultimate sin.

To have higher expectations of relationships is good but it also means we have become very self-critical. We measure how we are doing. We worry about how the people who mean so much to us think we are doing. This makes us insecure. Previous generations had enough on their hands just *surviving*; I doubt they felt under as much pressure of this sort – and this extra pressure often betrays itself in our body language.

Pressure to perform

Sex is one of life's great joys. Because it reveals so much of our true self, because it opens us up to someone else, it also makes most of us nervous.

It is especially stressful (though few of us have the confidence to speak about it) now that we are meant to be really good at sex. Until recently, sex was not seen – or at least not written about – as a performance art. There was so much unhealthy shame and embarrassment about sexuality that no one discussed the finer points of technique. Men wanted sex. Women were meant not to, but let men have their evil way with them out of love. They closed their eyes and thought of England. There was not an orgasm-o-meter running in your head measuring your performance in bed – or that of your partner.

It's different now, however.

We know when we go out with someone that they have done this before. Children of twelve in the United States see themselves as 'dating'. When I was a teenager, my cousin gave me a book called *The Art of Dating*. It had handy tips on how to order a burger for your beloved but carefully avoided anything physical. You respected your date too much for anything like *that*. The latest surveys suggest that in Britain 43% of boys have lost their virginity by the age of 16; 38% of girls by the age of 16.

As relationships progress, we disclose more and more about ourselves to the person we are 'seeing'. But such disclosures take time and trust. The first time we go out with someone, we are likely to have many unspoken – and unspeakable – anxieties. Typical ones would be:

- 'Does he/she really like me?'
- 'What does he/she expect of the evening?'
- 'Do I look good?'
- 'What kind of person is he/she?'

Some of these questions cause a great deal of worry. Learning body language will not make all your problems disappear, but it does offer

Figure 10 *A contemporary but classic female pose. This woman is waiting. Her posture is receptive, not aggressive. She is wearing what looks like a gender-bending outfit but is in fact gamine and very feminine.*

Figure 9 *The Stiff Man, tight military posture.*

important clues to knowing how you feel and how those around you feel, and this will help you understand the relationships you are in better.

In this book, I want to concentrate on body language in relationships. In Chapter 2, I look at the basics of body language. In Chapter 3, I look at what is important about first impressions. In Chapter 4, I look at first dates. In Chapter 5, I look at making love for the first time with a new partner and at sex in established relationships. In Chapter 6, I look at how body language can tell us when things start to go wrong. Finally, in Chapter 7 we review the progress we have made.

Some people seem naturally perceptive. Many

Figure 11 *Here the woman's look is much more dominant and assertive. Her posture proclaims that she is in control.*

of us feel we really don't understand what other people are thinking. No one needs to feel at such a disadvantage. And there is a final point to learning about body language. You will learn to observe *yourself*, and to get to know what you are like better than you thought possible.

Where you start from

It's always useful when studying a new skill to get a sense of where you are starting from. There are no right or wrong answers to the following questions but they should give you some sense of how much you already notice – or fail to notice – about body language:

1: How aware are you of the way the gestures that other people make:
Very aware   Somewhat aware   Hardly notice
2: List five things that you like about the way you think others see you.
3: List five things that you dislike about the way you think others see you.
4: Roughly how long did it take you to make the lists for Questions 2 and 3?
5: You have gone for a shortish train journey. Do you spend most of your time
   (i) reading a book
   (ii) looking at the scenery
   (iii) looking at the faces of the other passengers
   (iv) planning what you do when you get to your destination
6: Do you ever make up stories about people you don't know – like the other passengers in the train?
7: Try to picture your best friend. What are his/her four most characteristic gestures?
8: Try to picture how you look to others. What are your four most characteristic gestures?

9: When you go out with someone, what is the thing you most notice about them:
  (i)   their clothes
  (ii) their smile
  (iii) their chat-up line
  (iv) the way they dance.

10: Do you find you can tell the mood your boyfriend/girlfriend is in:
  (i)   usually
  (ii) quite often
  (iii) some of the time
  (iv) he/she always surprises you.

(As I said, there are no right or wrong answers to these questions. Guidelines that will help you to interpret your answers are given in Chapter 7.)

Imagine

Another thing worth thinking about is what it would be like to have absolutely no idea of body language. The following might happen . . .

You go to a meeting. Someone sticks out their hand for you to shake and you do a somersault . . .

You are trying to have a conversation. Since you can't read any body language at all, you don't pick up the signals that say: 'It's your turn to speak'. Everyone lapses into awkward silence . . .

You go to a restaurant. Since you are a Body Language Disaster Area, you lean back in your chair and put your feet on the table, spilling wine over your date. Well, that's another relationship gone! . . .

Your boyfriend is crying. Since you're blind to body language you don't know what that means, and you start singing and dancing, doing your latest Madonna impersonation . . .

All these scenarios are ridiculous. No one could survive without some sense of body language. But most of us know far less than we think we know, and, often, we don't use what we do know because we don't pay enough attention to it.

The point of asking the questions 1-10 is that they show how we need to *concentrate* in order to pick up the body language that's presented to us all the time.

Now, back to basics.

2

The Basics of Body Language

In Oscar Wilde's famous comedy, *The Importance of Being Earnest* Lady Bracknell asks the man who wants to marry her daughter:

'Do you know everything or nothing, Mr Worthing?'

'I know nothing, Lady Bracknell.'

Lady Bracknell approves. 'Ignorance is like a delicate exotic fruit; touch it and the bloom is gone.'

In the hundred years since Lady Bracknell made this observation, doctors and scientists have come to the opposite conclusion. Ignorance about sex causes much pain and suffering. It can destroy relationships. Many people feel so embarrassed about personal problems they are unable to talk about them.

Couples who start a relationship usually find it hard to discuss sex – and this is often reflected in their body language. Couples find it hard to admit to each other that there are things they don't know. To confess you don't know the meaning of a sexual word, for instance, can make you feel hopelessly foolish and inexperienced. Ignorance hinders rather than helps relationships.

The sexologists

Though most human beings are fascinated by sex, scientists who study it have usually met with resistance. They have often been accused of being immoral.

The last twenty-five years have seen a huge increase in scientific research into sexual behaviour. We know a lot more about what happens to our bodies when we are aroused. We have mapped the physiology of foreplay and intercourse. Nevertheless, sexologists often complain of their lot. Fellow academics dismiss them as dirty old scientists; their subjects want to be romantically involved with them; the media look for scandal; and the public have lurid fantasies about what goes on in their laboratories. Sexology is no picnic.

In the 1870s the German psychiatrist Richard Krafft-Ebing catalogued every variety of sexual activity. His book, *Psychopathia Sexualis*, had to be published in Latin so that only doctors would understand it. Sigmund Freud was often attacked. After one lecture in Vienna, in which he claimed that children are sexual beings, legend had it that some of his audience (all of them doctors) tried to summon the police. That tale has turned out to be an exaggeration, but Freud was certainly often treated as a dangerous outcast peddling a wicked theory.

Stages of sexual development

Freud argued that adult sexual behaviour depends on childhood experiences. He claimed children had sexual feelings well before puberty. He argued that children go through *oral, anal* and *genital* phases of development.

Freud weaved these observations into a theory of the development of sexuality. Babies get pleasure from the mouth. They suck at the nipple: they stick anything they can find between their lips. Memories of that pleasure stay with us and are often evoked again during adult sexual behaviour.

The next stage is the anal stage. Toddlers go

through a time when they are entranced by potties, toilets and the waste products of their body. In my Ph.D thesis, I studied what makes young children laugh. I found that 'pooh-pooh' jokes were a constant source of delight to eighteen-month-olds. Merely to utter the magic words 'pooh-pooh' would send most children under twenty-four months into hysterical giggles.

The next stage is the genital one. Young children touch their private parts. They are fascinated with 'willies' and 'fannies' and show them off proudly to each other. The Victorians liked to believe in the innocence of children. They often punished children who touched themselves. To them, ideas like Freud's seemed truly shocking.

Around the age of seven children enter the latency stage. They stop being sexual. Freud argued that boys realise they can't fulfil their deepest unconscious desire – to marry their mother and replace their father. The only way to cope is to put their sexuality on ice till puberty reawakens it.

Freud has been heavily criticised by other psychologists but his theories remain influential. They highlight the unconscious element in sexual desires. Sex is surrounded by taboos and secrets. No wonder it makes many people neurotic or nervous. Our body language often reflects these conscious and unconscious anxieties.

Losing our ignorance

In 1938, the year before Freud died, an American expert on insects, Alfred Kinsey, was asked to give a series of lectures on sexual behaviour. Kinsey was amazed to find there were no reliable data on normal sexual behaviour in the US. For the next ten years he interviewed over two thousand people, eventually producing *Sexual Behaviour in the Human Male* (1948, the so-called 'Kinsey Report') and *Sexual Behaviour in the Human Female* (1953). Kinsey became controversial for the same reasons Freud had been. His painstaking research showed that people were less moral than they liked to believe. Kinsey found most Americans had had some experience of sex outside marriage, and that nearly 50 per cent of American girls were not virgins when they married. America was shocked but fascinated.

Even in the so-called 'swinging sixties', when two American researchers, William Masters and Virginia Johnson, studied the physiology of love-making they met a huge amount of opposition. Masters and Johnson did go further than anyone before. They observed couples making love to order and monitored their physiological responses. Lady Bracknell would have been shocked.

We owe much to these pioneers because we are now infinitely less ignorant than Lady Bracknell would have liked. Ignorance isn't really a delicate exotic fruit but a recipe for disaster.

Arousal

Our bodies are soft machines flowing with electricity, biochemicals and hormones. Changes in the levels of these can now be measured. Techniques also exist that make it possible to monitor brain waves, heart rate, pulse, blood pressure, breathing rate and the galvanic skin response which reflects the electricity in the skin. These measures produce a cluster of responses. They tend to vary together. It's possible to distinguish three states of the organism:

The first stage, sleep, is the lowest level of arousal (see figure 12).

The next stage is normal arousal. You are

Figure 12 *Low level of arousal*

Figure 13 *Normal arousal*

Figure 14 *High arousal*

17

awake, alert, but nothing much is going on (see (figure 13).

The third stage is high arousal (see figure 14). You wake up and remember you have a terrifying interview with your boss who is not happy with your work.

In many ways the particular emotion you feel does not matter. As long as it is intense, the following symptoms of high arousal will be found:

• the heart beats more quickly
• the pulse rate is faster
• blood pressure rises
• the galvanic skin response rises
• reflexes are quicker

The pattern of these changes isn't accidental. They allow our body to react more swiftly to survive. When aroused, the body will produce the hormones adrenalin and noradrenalin which help increase heart action and the release of glucose. There is some evidence that when presented with attractive stimuli there is a slow release of sexual hormones: testosterone in men and oestrogen in women.

Ironically, love and fear produce many of the same physiological reactions. In 1962, in a famous experiment, Singer and Schachter gave subjects injections of epinephrine. The subjects became highly aroused. They were put in a waiting room. They thought the main experiment was to come, a series of tests. In fact the crucial point was to see what subjects said they felt depending on who came to sit with them in the waiting room. Some subjects sat with a friendly stooge; others with a person feigning aggression. The quality of the encounter determined what subjects felt. Those who met a happy person felt joyful; those who met an aggressive one felt angry. All that being physiologically aroused did was to prime subjects to feel intensely.

Sexual arousal has many of the characteristics of other strong emotions like fear. But it has its own particular points. Men usually don't get erections when they are afraid!

Many things can lead to sexual arousal – a lovely face, a smell, a conversation in which you feel drawn closer and closer, a joke, a picture or a tone of voice. Men respond more to visual stimuli and/or pornography, though that may now be changing. Some women now feel free to be turned on by sex objects. Twenty years ago there may have been the odd male stripper but he was treated as a girls'-night-out joke. Now acts like the Chippendales attract huge audiences and many women happily admit that hunks turn them on. The male has become a sex object too.

Humans are the only species to be nearly always ready for sex. Our sexual cycles may affect how randy we feel but only to a minor extent. We are not so much the naked ape as the randy ape.

Erotic surfaces

Any part of the body can be erotic. As relationships develop, people show off to one another more and more intimate parts of their body. Studies of body language show that we like to make much of our erotic surfaces and that, as we reveal and display them, we play many games. We decorate our eyes, our ears, our lips, our wrists to show off how seductive we are. As we get close to someone we let them see more and more of our body. The sexologists concentrate on the genitals; there is much more to intimate body language than that.

The face

Show a two-month-old baby a cardboard cut-out like 'A' and they will probably smile. Show them a

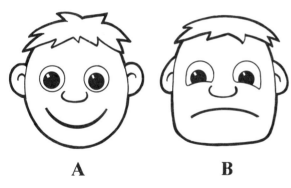

A   **B**

Figure 15

face like 'B' and they may well cry or react with fear (see figure 15). Some psychologists argue that because babies show these reactions when they are so young, the skill to tell a happy face from a sad face must be genetically 'hard wired'

into us. And for good reason. The face conveys vital social and emotional signals. Infants need to learn as soon as possible how to 'read' these signals.

The mouth

People speak of 'sensual mouths', of 'tight-lipped' people, or of people with 'stiff upper lips'. The shape of the mouth is as irrelevant as the shape of

Figure 16 *The muscles of the face shape the expressions, the smiles and the contour of the mouth. These form constantly shifting patterns which we have to interpret.*

19

the nose. What matters is how the mouth is used. Is it used defensively, clamped shut against the assaults of the world? Or is it relaxed, ready to open? The brain devotes a great deal of processing space to sensations from around the mouth, more than to any other part of the body other than the genitals.

To remind yourself how sensitive your mouth is, touch it. Run a finger along the lips, on your tongue, just inside your mouth.

Alert babies have this expression on their faces (figure 17). It means they are concentrating hard on what is happening in front of them. Adults are more subtle, but one sign of alertness is still a slightly opened mouth, with lips in perfect position to say: 'Oh'.

Normally, unless we are speaking, our lips are closed. But closed mouths can be either firmly clamped shut against the world, or more relaxed, not even half open but prepared to open (figure 18).

Mouths become much more active and mobile in intimate settings. The lips relax when you are comfortable. They part slightly. This is a sensuous

Figure 17 *The Open Mouth 'Oh' Look*

20

Figure 18 *The closed mouth. Here she also uses her fingers as an extra guard.*

Figure 19 *The open lips suggest intimacy and openness. She reinforces that impression by putting her hand very close to her heart as if to say 'I really am speaking the truth – from the heart'.*

position which is emphasised when people have their fingers close to their mouths (figure 19).

Adults often come close to thumb-sucking. It is intimate and erotic but also suggests insecurity. Putting the finger to the mouth and even just sucking or gnawing a finger tip is comforting because it's often the way we reassured ourselves when we were small children. It shows how Freud's oral phase where we sucked everything for love and comfort never quite fades away (see figures 20 and 21).

The tongue

The tongue is an organ we don't usually see a lot of. To show your tongue to someone is either intimate, aggressive or a combination of the two.

Sticking the tongue out at someone is either meant to insult them or make them laugh. We also unconsciously allow the tongue to 'fidget'

Figure 20 *The fingers touch the mouth but the lips don't open. This suggests that you are assessing the person or situation before you.*

Figure 21 *The fingers touch the mouth and are inserted very slightly into the open lips. This is a watchful but slightly erotic pose.*

when we feel worried. Common acts of tongue-worrying include touching the back of the teeth or lips with the tongue. Some people combine this with pulling at their lips. Touching oneself, making sure you are still there, is a basic form of human comfort.

The smile

Smiling conveys many different messages. The face has many muscles, and surprisingly the muscles used to smile appear to differ depending on whether the smile is sincere or not. If you could X-ray the face of the person smiling at you and check whether they were using a muscle known as the *risorius* muscle 12, you would always know whether the smile was sincere. Most people don't have X-ray eyes so you need to learn to read the quick signals that flutter across the face to make different smiles.

The *sincere* smile (see figure 22) is well-rounded,

Figure 22 *The Sincere Smile*

slow to develop, slow to fade, involving the risorius muscle 12. Both sides of the face look alike. This is the symmetrical smile.

The smile that is too long and abruptly cut off is probably *insincere* (see figure 23). It becomes lopsided and asymmetrical.

The *nervous* smile is usually too short and cut off.

The laugh

I have found there are at least fourteen reasons why children laugh. These range from lording it over a weaker child, to mastering a skill, to celebrating a bond. Adults are just as complex. Freud argued that jokes allow us to raise sexual subjects that would otherwise be taboo.

When she laughs with her head thrown back a woman is laying herself open, revealing her neck.

In a non-sexual laugh (for example, figure 24), the rest of the body remains well controlled. No surface is thrown back.

The eyes

Romantic literature makes much of the eyes, their colour, their intensity, their power – and with good reason.

The eyes change in size and dilation when we become sexually attracted to someone. Two people who are attracted to each other will make more eye contact than another couple. They will get in a position to look at each other more and there will be more rhythm to their gaze. American men report that one of the features they find physically most attractive are women with large eyes set widely apart. Women too often speak of how attractive large eyes are.

Relative to the size of their bodies, babies' eyes are very large. It looks as if we are wired to

Figure 23 *Here the woman is not looking at the man as she is smiling. Note too her slightly lopsided head position, again suggesting a lack of ease and sincerity in the encounter.*

Figure 24 *The dynamics of this group laugh are interesting. We are in a work situation – not a sexual one. One woman has made a joke. The others do not laugh, however. Only one man laughs – his head slightly thrown back, his lips open.*

respond positively to adults who look like babies – the kind of finding that would have delighted Freud.

Looking at someone you desire feels good but looking for too long overstimulates the nervous system and can appear to be threatening. When a couple are attracted to each other, there is a typical pattern of gaze. Each looks at the other and then looks away. It's easy to see that they daren't stare too long, not because it's rude but because it's overstimulating.

To get a contrast, imagine what it is like trying to catch a waiter's eye. Here there is much less problem about staring: the wonder is how he avoids eye contact.

Clusters

The eyes, the mouth, smiles and laughter all reveal a great deal of what we feel and the fantasies that underlie it. We move our eyes, mouths, bodies in a co-ordinated way. To understand body language well you have to understand not only single gestures (though as we shall see these often have a

Figure 25 *Eye make up accentuates the size of the eyes.*

Figure 26 *The man is trying very hard to justify himself for something. He is leaning forward, his fist is clenched, his face tenses around his mouth. He seems to be saying he's sorry. The gesture of his hand and mouth, together with his tight posture, form an apologetic, pleading cluster of body language. The woman provides a perfect foil. She is leaning forward, emphasizing that he's made a mistake.*

meaning) but *clusters* of gestures and small micro-signals like the slight tremor on the lips when very nervous. Figure 26 shows an example of clusters in action.

Throughout this book, I'll be analysing clusters of body language.

Sexual arousal

When two people go out for the first time together, both are likely to imagine what it might be like to have a relationship. Each is likely to have fantasies about what it would be like to touch and be touched by the other person. Masters and Johnson found that such imaginings had a very direct effect on sexual physiology.

In every culture people cover their genitals. When European explorers travelled to remote parts of the earth, they found few places where there wasn't some such clothing. They thought this reflected the universal sense of shame humankind had been saddled with ever since we were exiled from the garden of Eden. It certainly reflects how important our sexual anatomy is.

One reason men and women have always covered their sexual parts is of course protection. The second reason is that we find nakedness highly arousing. It's not surprising that men find the sight of female breasts erotic. They are bound to evoke deep memories of being held and fed as a baby.

In the 1960s, Masters and Johnson revolutionised our knowledge of sex. In their lab, they wired up volunteers and got precise readings of what was happening when they were aroused and when they made love. The studies were controversial but enlightening.

Masters and Johnson argued that both sexes need to understand their own anatomy and that of their partners. Where and how you touch can lead to either exquisite pleasure or frustration. It isn't always easy to know just what you are touching.

They put forward a theory that there are four stages in sexual activity. The first stage is *arousal*. This is marked by high pulse rate, quickened breathing, the start of erection in the male, tingly feelings in the female and, psychologically, a slightly heady feeling. When a couple are both aroused, they will want to make love. Sexual pleasure is unlike other kinds of pleasure because foreplay is so important. Part of the delight of

making love is building up tension and waiting, waiting, waiting for release. Some Eastern texts on love-making recommend ways of making foreplay last for hours before intercourse.

Most lovers are not so patient, but still try to make each other more and more excited. Foreplay gives pleasure in itself and also ensures greater pleasure and 'satisfaction'.

This growing excitement leads to the *plateau* stage. It is a plateau because most women – and some men – have to spend some time highly excited before they can reach orgasm. For men, the problem is often not to climax too soon. For women, the problem tends to be that it takes a long time in the plateau stage to get close to orgasm.

The third stage is orgasm. Orgasm has many similarities in both men and women. It is a reaction of the whole body, a release of psychological and physiological tension. Orgasms consist of rhythmical muscular contractions and don't last long.

The final and fourth stage is *resolution*. The tension has been discharged: we remain slightly aroused but do not need to have sex. Then, slowly, the body returns to its normal state. Despite the legend that after men make love they then roll over and go to sleep, Masters and Johnson found few instances of that.

Studies of sex education in Britain repeatedly show that teachers find the subject embarrassing and so give pupils only very partial information. Few parents find it easy to talk about sex to their children. Everyone assumes you know 'the facts of life', yet the facts of life are complex and it's far from clear who will tell you about them. The problems we have in teaching children about sex reflect the many taboos that surround the subject – taboos that affect adults and often embarrass them. It means we often enter relationships unaware of many things we should know – something which is worrying.

If you grasp the basics of body language – and that includes knowing the basics of sex – you have a much better chance of making relationships work for you. In Chapter 3 I will look at how relationships start and what you need to do to make a good first impression on those you want to impress.

3

First Impressions

Most of us know that parties are not the best place to get to know anyone. There's too much noise, too much showing off and just too much going on.

Yet parties are often precisely where we do see someone across a crowded room. Through the chatter of flirting and all that competing for attention, you catch someone looking at you. What will determine your first impression?

Much will depend on their face and their smile. We tend to rate symmetrical faces as beautiful and symmetrical smiles as sincere. If the look they give you is a leering grin or a tight, lop-sided

Figure 27 *The couple are leaning towards each other, showing their manifest liking for each other at the start of a date. The mirroring is obvious but positive.*

smile, you're likely to turn away even though you won't know why you're doing it.

For over forty years psychologists have been puzzled by why first impressions can matter so much. Many of us have experienced the odd feeling of liking someone the moment we meet them. It's not love at first sight but liking at first sight.

In 1979 an American psychologist, Robert Zajonc, argued that such immediate liking was the product of 'hot cognitions'. A hot cognition is a belief that has a strong emotional component attached.

The first few seconds of an encounter are crucial, Zajonc found. It's then that people 'decide' whether or not they like someone, even though they know they don't know enough to make a reasonable judgment. Our instincts outstrip our intelligence (see figure 27).

Zajonc can't explain exactly what is going on in these powerful first moments but it is probably a matter of *non-verbal communication*. Some people's styles of non-verbal communication mesh: others clash.

Inexplicable but true! When you meet Joe, immediately, you want to spend time with him – or her. When you meet Freddie, you *know* he or she's a horrible creep, or a ghastly woman. You think there's no logic to it but there *is* a kind of psycho-logic to it.

What makes people attractive?

In most cultures, people agree on who is and who is not physically attractive. But what features make someone attractive in the West? American college men judge women attractive who have these 'cute' characteristics:

• large and widely separated eyes

Figure 28 *We are at a wedding. George is holding himself stiffly, a classic masculine position. Sarah is much less stiff, suggesting she is out for rather more frivolity than he can offer.*

• small nose
• small chin

These are all features that mimic the looks of small children. Other attractive features – wide cheekbones and narrow cheeks – are not at all childlike.

We also tend to find people attractive if we see them as intelligent and if they share similar attitudes to ours.

Conflicting styles

George and Sarah should like each other, but their first meeting is a wash out and will probably be their last.

As you can see from figure 28, George's body language is confident but businesslike. George has shaken hands with Sarah and has retreated to a formal distance. He stands quite stiffly. When he talks, he emphasises points with little stabs, as if he's at a board meeting. Sarah, however, wants fun at this party. She's dressed for frivolity. She wants to amuse and be amused. Her stance is more relaxed. This is a perfect mismatch.

Different kinds of personality try to attract the opposite sex in very different ways. According to the psychologist Hans Eysenck, you can rank people's personality styles on a continuum from extraverted to introverted. You can see it at any party. The extrovert loves the social whirl. He acts confidently, enjoys talking to people of both sexes, and likes cracking jokes. He exudes bonhomie. The introvert has problems with parties. He is shyer, worried about the impression he might make. Conflicting personality styles and body languages can easily lead to problems.

Figure 29 *A confident but not over-dominant man shaking hands with a woman. He faces her but doesn't try to dominate. He doesn't grip her hand too long. He looks her in the eyes but not for too long. If he is interested, he will do nothing too sudden. A stable extrovert.*

Saying Hello

The way you greet a stranger of the opposite sex can range from a curt nod with no physical contact to taking their hand and kissing it like a knight of old (see figures 29–32).

The confident woman doesn't wait for the man to speak but says who she is and what she's doing there. She has taken on many classic masculine traits. On the other hand there's the shy type. Wallflowers can be male or female. They don't like shaking hands and may just nod. Some

Figure 30 *The dominant male. He shakes hands at an angle. He shows her less of his body than she shows him. He holds her hand a long time, as if he is feeling the texture of her skin. He glances up and down her, not lecherously but assessing how good her clothes, make up and jewellery are. He likes to be in control but he is too aware of his status to make a crass pass at a party. After the party, in private, he may well be much less inhibited.*

Figure 31 *The show off. The 'cock of the walk' preens rather obviously. He thrusts his chest out, his crotch is slightly forward and he puts his hand on her shoulder which implies he owns his partner. He wins The Most Likely to Make a Crass Pass Award. In some Latin cultures such preening is more acceptable than in Anglo-Saxon ones. Such men may actually take the hand of a perfect stranger and kiss them like an old-style knight. Nice women don't giggle too much at this display. This man is a high extravert.*

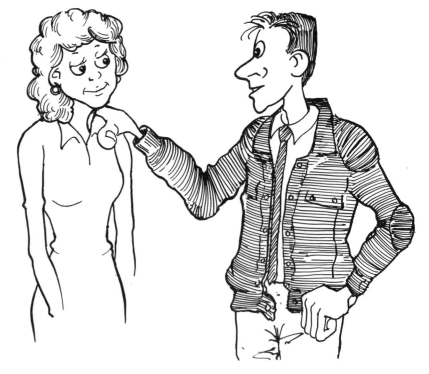

Figure 32
'I'm too good to be here so I'm not going to come down to your level' – or even bother to talk to you.

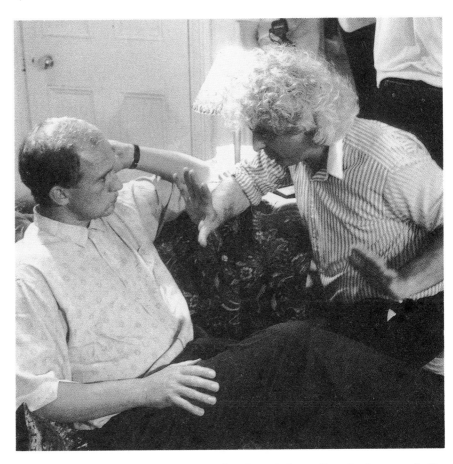

introverts find physical contact difficult.

There are also shy-aggressive men who retreat from too much contact. Often they seem meek but actually they believe they are superior to all around. At parties they refuse to get involved but deliver a sardonic commentary on what is happening from the sidelines.

'Hot cognitions'

Stiff George did not get on well with Relaxed Sarah. But a much more positive encounter is that between Sarah and Sam. Sam looks casual. He catches Sarah's attention first by tugging her sleeve and smiling. His smile is very positive.

They start talking and get on well. Is it just because they're interested in the same kinds of things? Probably not. Unconscious factors almost certainly affect their feelings. Positive 'hot cognitions' may occur when two people's body language meshes – and we can mesh in many different ways.

Once women were expected to be submissive.

Now they don't have to play to those old rules (see figures 33 and 34).

Body language also expresses attempts to dominate and, traditionally, one way men compete is by getting the attention of the most attractive woman around. But there are different styles:

The *lout* tries to achieve dominance by boasting, talking loud, and putting his arms around a number of girls. Some like it.

The *clown* has found that a good way of getting attention is to tell funny stories. The more people listen to you, the more attention you get.

Figure 33 *This woman ignores the 'cock of the walk' tactics of Macho Man. She has turned half away and is presenting very little of her body to him. Her hand is at an angle away from him indicating she's looking to make contact with someone else.*

Does he/she like me?

We want to be liked not only by the people we like, but by the people we *don't* like. But how can you tell whether you are liked by either?

In *Star Trek*, the Starship Enterprise uses the services of a Betazoid empath, who can read other people's minds. In battle, this gives the crew a great psychological advantage. At most earth parties we can't rely on mind-reading – but we can do a spot of body-reading.

When someone is paying attention to you it will

Figure 34 *Using the sofa. One ploy people can use at parties to achieve dominance is to hog the slightly higher end of the sofa. Power-dressed madam here is very skilled at this.*

show in their posture, in their tone of voice, in the way they look at you and in the signals they give to show they are listening to you.

We can use our bodies to receive or to block people. The most obvious block is to turn your back to someone. But there are subtler blocks, such as half-turning towards or away from

Figure 35 *The two men seem absorbed in their own conversation, and totally uninterested in the girl in the middle. Interpret this behaviour with care, though – they might just be putting on a performance to show her how sophisticated they are!*

someone or, when you are sitting with them, staring out into the middle distance beyond them. Both these postures make it harder for eye contact to occur.

It is normal for people to look, to look away and then look again. On the whole the ratio of time spent looking directly at people should be about two-thirds. This should be interspersed with shorter periods during which you look away and then look back at them.

Someone interested in you will look at your face and eyes. If the situation is potentially sexual, they are also likely to look covertly at your body. Skilled men manage to look at a woman's body, but they do so in quick little flurries, without staring. They will do so more while they are talking, because then the woman opposite should be concentrating on their lips. If she's looking at their lips, she's less likely to catch them out looking down her front. When women look at men they tend to focus on faces, chests and shoulders. They look at the crotch area less than men do, but then

Figure 36 *Styles of good listening. The head is forward. The hands are often in play and pointing towards the other person. In a romantic situation the listener may have a finger near his nose and lips. He's concentrating and aware of the possibility of touch.*

sexually interested men tend to nudge their crotch forward.

Someone is not paying attention to you if the amount of time they spend looking at you is significantly less than the amount of time they spend scanning away. Often, distracted behaviour will be accompanied by asymmetrical smiles and nervous head turns. At work-related parties it's not polite to scan the horizon for others to talk to, but it may be inevitable. People have to see who else is there. At a real party, the restless scanner is giving a negative message. He or she just doesn't want to know you. Console yourself with the thought that they're self-centred (see figure 35).

The second way of telling if someone is paying attention to you is to notice if they are listening not just to what you say but to the rhythm of your conversation. When we listen we rely on small, specific cues to know when it is our turn to speak next. Non-verbal signals are vital for conversation to flow. Good listeners instinctively know how to encourage speakers by focused looking, small nods of the head and brief smiles. To send the unspoken message 'I want to speak', a listener turns his or her head away, gestures definitely and inhales. Good listeners do this when someone is coming to the end of a clause, to signal they want to butt in and speak (see figure 36). Some feminists argue that women are much better listeners than men, but it may be that women just give more explicit feedback to men than men do to women.

One way men can improve their listening skills is to learn this kind of body language and put it into practice. You will find that if you manage to maintain these kinds of position, you will start to listen more empathically. And women like men who listen well (see figure 37).

Look closely at the mouth of the person who is listening to you. The mouth should be relaxed,

Figure 37
The extroverted Good Listener may often place his hands behind his neck. This mimics a really open pose saying: 'Tell me. All my body is listening to you.'

Figure 38
Crude mirroring. Her hands are folded behind her so he does the same.

fairly still. It should not be asymmetrical. Mouth asymmetry reflects discomfort and nervousness. People who are self-absorbed often suck their lips, rub their tongue along the back of their teeth or contort their lips. Another asymmetrical danger signal is that a listener who's bored will put their head on one side, or even prop it up with one hand or finger.

I have already pointed out the difference between slow symmetrical smiles and quick asymmetrical ones. The first kind of smile suggests real liking: the second kind of smile suggests mere politeness, at best.

One truly off-putting non-verbal signal is the Stifled Yawn, where someone shuts their mouth tight and puffs out air through their lips. You can see their cheeks balloon slightly as they do this.

Some techniques to practise

Controlling conversation

You can control interactions by encouraging the person who is speaking to you. If you nod, if you smile at them – especially if you smile when they pause – you will find they will talk more and feel you are a good listener.

This needs to be done subtly or the other person will feel you are trying to manipulate them.

Positions at parties

People who like each other stay close but not too close when they first get to know each other. They are aware of the need to respect each other's space and not be pushy. A simple little game is fun. Edge just a fraction nearer them and watch their response. Do they do nothing and pretend it never happened? Do they retreat? Or do they mirror your movement and edge just a shade closer to you?

Mirroring

Mirroring is a technique by which you imitate the body language of the person opposite you. The theory is that, if the mirroring is discreet, they will feel warm and positive towards you. As we have seen, we tend to like fairly similar people. In some situations the mirroring is very natural, as when two lovers lean towards each other. But in other situations, it can look crude and obvious (see figure 38). During the course of a conversation, for example, if you shift position every time the person you are talking to shifts it will look too obvious. But you can mirror sensitively. For example, you don't imitate the precise body moves of your partner but their general message. If it is that he is feeling warm – and you like it – you can generate more warmth by behaving similarly (see figure 39).

Some people think mirroring is a 'trick' and so become wary of those who do it. That's especially true in business situations. So be careful how you use it as a technique.

Lying

There is another form of conscious use of body language to impress. Argyle found there were a number of so-called 'Machiavellian subjects' who, when they lied, put out signals of great sincerity. They looked people straight in the eye, showed no tell-tale head shakes and lied through the back of their teeth.

Special problems

Special problems may occur when two people with different personality styles like each other but find it hard to adapt to each other's rhythms of interaction.

A man who sees himself as a sensitive 'new

Figure 39
Clever mirroring.
There is some mirroring
but it is not too obvious.

man' may refuse to act pushy. He may make a girl who is used to assertive men feel ugly. Why doesn't he make a move if he really likes me? An introverted man may feel threatened by a girl who shows early on that she expects public displays of affection.

Tom and Jenny

Relationships are complex, living things. An atlas of body language might be useful, but I'd like to flesh out some of these points by a case history which shows how being aware of body language can be a big help in building a good relationship.

A romance starts

Tom is twenty-four and a motorcycle messenger. Jenny is twenty-two and a receptionist. The first time Tom saw Jenny, he was delivering documents to her office. She was busy and didn't look up at him. Mechanically, she signed the docket.

Usually, Tom does not take off his helmet

RECEPTION

Figure 40 *Receptionists in offices are protected by desks which are often tall. You need to do something dramatic like leaning on it as if it were a bar to make it less defensive.*

when he goes into offices. He noticed Jenny, however. He thought she was very pretty. Tom wanted to say something cheerful, even vaguely flirtatious, but he didn't want to make a performance of taking his helmet off. With it on, he looks like a lumbering spaceman.

The next day, Tom delivered more documents. This time, he took his helmet off downstairs. He knew that if he could make eye contact with Jenny there was a better chance of getting something started. Jenny didn't realise that he was the man who had made the delivery yesterday.

'I don't usually take off my helmet,' Tom said, smiling.

'Entering a beauty contest are you?'

Jenny's snappy answer disconcerted him. Maybe she was hard despite his first impression.

'You look like an astronaut with that on,' she smiled.

Tom noticed her smile was quite long and not twitchy. But he wasn't confident enough to say anything more.

Men will understand Tom's predicament. Men usually still have to make the first move and, in doing so, they run the risk of rejection. How could Tom know whether suggesting they have a drink might be welcome?

Women will, I suspect, say: What do you expect Jenny to do? Grab his hand? Sit in a come-on pose?

Tom wasn't discouraged. He hadn't got very far but he was confident that Jenny's firm would have more documents delivered in the next few days.

41

Figure 41 *Tom looms over Jenny. 'You have got to want me. I'm Arnold Schwarzenegger Mark 2.'*

Jenny was surprised Tom hadn't said something nasty when she'd made her crack about the beauty contest. Most messengers were touchy, and planned glorious careers. Few liked being delivery boys.

Personal space

At the maybe start of a maybe relationship, people are sensitive to personal space. Arabs and Latins would think it rude to stay as far away as Tom.

Tom, however, isn't a Latin or an Arab. He might have sat on Jenny's desk and loomed over her. It would have given him a chance to get really close to her and to gaze, as he wants to, at her breasts. But Tom is quite sensitive, so he's stayed at a friendly distance. Close enough to suggest he is interested but not so close as to be oppressive.

Women often complain about too-pushy men who invade their personal space.

If Tom had come as close as in figure 41, Jenny would have felt threatened. Office furniture often provides ideal defensive props for women. There is the head-down-and-on-to-the-word-processor move. There is the total-concentration-on-the-telephone move. There is also the 'my-only-love-is-the-photocopying-machine' response. All these can be used to deflect office Romeos.

When our personal space is invaded we find it unpleasant. In the London underground or the New York or Tokyo subway at rush hour, people are squashed close to perfect strangers. Normally you would only be so close to someone if you were going to kiss them. Human beings have their defences. In the tube, passengers allow their eyes to glaze over. The look says: 'I am not really here', 'I am being transported', 'No one inside'. Introverts find it harder to cope with the invasion of personal space than do extraverts.

The first move

Making the first move is always risky. You might be told to clear off. Some men respond to such insecurity by being over-aggressive.

Tom, however, is relaxed, and he has a good sense of body language. It's lucky he doesn't do anything too aggressive, because Jenny loathes macho men. She had enough of that with one of her first boyfriends.

As Tom stands there Jenny realises that he is quite nice looking. His patter is amusing and he seems quite relaxed. She thinks he has a nice smile, though she doesn't realise that's because it's highly symmetrical.

'Can you sign for them please?'

Tom hands Jenny his docket for her to sign. They are brought closer by this move and, during it, they smile at each other again. There was a time when Jenny's friendly smile would have seemed outrageously forward. In Marivaux's eighteenth-century classic play *Infidelities*, Arlequin, a country lad, describes his courtship of Silvia:

If I told you the story of our love, how you'd admire her modesty. At first she would back away when I came near her. Then she would back away less and then, little by little, she didn't back away any more. She looked at me stealthily, and when I saw her she would blush with shame. And I felt like a king when I saw how ashamed she was of looking at me.

Today, Silvia's behaviour would be seen as a bit precious and over-shy.

Tom and Jenny are not eighteenth-century rustics. They have looked and liked what they have seen. Like a typical man, Tom has looked not just at Jenny's face but down her body. Like a typical woman, Jenny has taken in the fact that he has big shoulders. She also likes the colour of his hair.

Tom's mobile phone buzzes but before he takes it he smiles at Jenny and makes a slightly pleading hand gesture.

It's a date

Tom has decided he needs to do something definite to show Jenny he wants to meet. The next time he delivers documents, he tells her: 'There's one just for you.'

It's a card from 'A helmet'. It's an invitation to have a drink. Cleverly, Tom retreats while she opens it. He isn't being pushy.

'I'll have to think about it,' Jenny says.

'Oh.' Tom is disappointed. He thought she'd say Yes at once. He doesn't know Jenny is having a relationship with Danny. Danny seems to take her for granted but Jenny hasn't quite given up on him. Tom covers up well. He smiles, trying hard not to cut short his smile.

'Nothing heavy. Just a drink.' Then he leaves quickly.

Jenny is relieved. She hates being under pressure.

The next day, Tom gets a message. Jenny's firm wants documents picked up and they want him to do it.

'Are you still offering that drink,' Jenny smiles. They both smile.

It will be weeks before Tom learns that what decided Jenny was Danny's behaviour the evening after Tom first asked her. Danny came round to her flat at 10.30, a lot the worse for drink, ate

Figure 42 *The arm extended, palm upwards. With a shrug and a smile, this means 'I want to continue this but can't now'. It's part of something we shall explore in the next chapter: The Approach-Avoidance Twostep.*

most of her fudge ice cream and got straight into bed expecting to make love. Danny the lout has made Tom's day.

Hostility and disclosure

Let's go back to our party. In one group, there's a couple who are arguing with each other. Sexual relationships often involve a good deal of aggression. Boy and girl may meet, fight and resist. Neither will admit they're attracted. They excite each other but they interpret that arousal as hostile, not erotic. In many movies, the plot hinges on how the boy and girl slowly realise they don't want to fight but to make love. Real life is often less dramatic, but at parties couples often circle around each other before opening a relationship. In this context the body language is partly sexual, partly aggressive. Some, like pinching someone's bottom, is obviously hostile-erotic. Conversations full of repartee peppered with slightly hostile and challenging stares show similar tensions in a nicer way.

If you feel hostile, you tend not to reveal too much about yourself – and parties make that easy. It's all gloss: lots of show and little tell. But the arousal is exciting. As you get less hostile, you disclose more – and a relationship starts. The more we go out with someone, the more we feel we like them, the more we say about our work, our family, our ambitions, our past relationships and our hopes for the future.

As we shall see in Chapter 4, as we reveal things about our lives, we tend to reveal parts of our bodies.

First impressions matter. Whether or not you get the chance to have a relationship with someone depends crucially on that first meeting.

If you want to know whether someone might want to go out with you, listen to what they have to say but also pay attention to their tone of voice, their gestures and how they look at you.

4

First Date, First Kiss

First dates would make an excellent subject for a Ph.D thesis. On a first date, we reveal our hopes, fantasies, and fears. It would be fascinating to examine exactly what happens when two people go out for the first time.

Being aware of your date's body language – and your own – will make it easier to understand what your potential partner is thinking, feeling and wants to do. Perhaps, as important, it tells you what they *don't* want and allows you to pace your 'interaction' in a way that is comfortable and enjoyable for both of you.

First dates can go badly wrong, often because of nerves or a conflict of expectations.

First dates have a clear agenda. You are trying to get to know each other, to see if you want to know each other. Both of you will be trying to impress the other. On first dates, people want to show they are attractive, intelligent, witty, sexy and interesting. The combination makes for fun – and nerves.

First date nerves

Recognising signs of your own nervousness is important. Freud found that anxious people often made 'Freudian slips' or unconscious errors. If you are unconsciously worried about how a date will work out, you might forget where and when you are meeting. The date can't go wrong if it doesn't happen. Your unconscious has 'protected' you by a slip of memory. You should be aware of its little stratagems!

Another sign of nerves is *repetition compulsion*. The repeated mirror check – going back to the

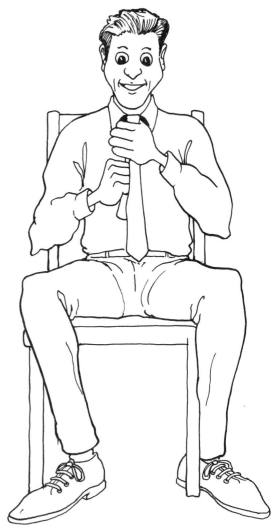

Figure 43 *Adjusting clothes. Men who are nervous will fidget with their ties, cigarettes or their socks. These movements are partly preening, partly discharge of energy.*

46

mirror a number of times to check your hair, your make-up, your earrings, your smile and whether you've brushed your teeth – is a common symptom of this.

The person you are meeting will probably also be nervous. In some cultures people use objects like worry beads. Fiddling with them absorbs nervous energy. We don't have worry beads in Anglo-Saxon cultures so we have to create our own worry objects to fidget with, like glasses, watches, pencils and bags.

Different personality types will also express their anxieties in different ways (see figure 43). Extraverts will tend to show very restless behaviour as a sign of nerves. Introverts will be much more withdrawn.

Both sexes when anxious are likely to go in for self-touching. Touching ourselves is comforting. While waiting, people touch their arms, their bottoms, their necks and often engage in complex hand, head and eye moves. They rub their fingers together, examine their nails and scratch their ears or the side of their face.

There is an interesting gesture, characteristic of people waiting, where the hand is brought down in front of the eyes and the face scrunches up. This movement has a certain 'magical' quality – when you uncover your eyes, perhaps your date will be there! Or men may sweep their hand over their hair, part grooming, part restlessness.

If you have fixed to meet at a particular place, the anxious male often prowls around to see if his date is coming. Women who are waiting tend to be more defensive. One reason for that is that a woman waiting is a possible target for unwelcome pick-ups. This kind of pose is often to be seen at meeting-places like a station or outside a cinema. The 'glazed' look is a signal to other men to say: 'Leave me alone. I am not interested in being

Figure 44 *Woman with glazed look, arms folded or crossed, waiting in public place.*

approached' (see figure 44).

People are most effective when they are moderately aroused. If you aren't aroused at all, you will feel unmotivated. If you are *too* aroused, you will try too hard and probably make mistakes. On a first date, mistakes, especially mistakes due to insecurity, can leave you looking and feeling very foolish.

There are ways of relaxing before you go out that it is worth remembering:

1. Try not to have too many fantasies about what will happen. Too-romantic expectations make you very vulnerable. A first date is exploration, not consummation.
2. Give yourself plenty of time to get to your rendezvous, so that you don't arrive hot and bothered.
3. If you feel tense, don't pretend it will just go away. Do something about it. The most practical way is to control your breathing. Exhale deeply. Cleanse yourself with a deep breath. Then inhale slowly and regularly. A little deep breathing isn't a panacea but you can do it just about anywhere. Two or three minutes of deep breathing should produce a calmer frame of mind.

The greeting

It's much better to admit to yourself that you feel insecure than to try to cover it up. Mr Macho Brash is unlikely to make a good impression if the moment he sees his date, he demands contact and attention just to reassure himself. To show how confident he is, he slings his arm round her shoulder and kisses her. Brilliant! She's annoyed before three minutes are up. It sounds obvious, it *is* obvious, and yet people often do it.

Figure 45 *The Over-Eager Greeting. Tell-tale signs show she is not happy with the mega embrace. She doesn't reciprocate touching. Her eyes look away from him. Her legs are tight and unrelaxed.*

A *kiss on the cheek* when you meet carries quite different messages. It's affectionate, not demanding. But it's still important to watch the reaction you get (see figure 45). Does your partner kiss you on the cheek back? Do they smile? If they show any signs of tension it suggests they don't like to be touched in casual ways.

A second unthreatening touch is the *touch on the arm*. It is warm but not overtly sexual.

There are some very clear *distance messages* that men in particular need to look out for.

We can use our *arms and hands* to create barriers to contact (see figure 46).

Figure 46 *Using arms and hands to create barriers; the crossed legs, too, form a barrier.*

If a woman walks holding her hands or a man walks holding his hands behind his back, it makes touching impossible. So don't try to touch them. When people are sitting, the most obvious defensive pose is to cross their arms. This means that they are comforting themselves: it excludes you.

Objects, too, form a barrier. A woman who is keeping her bag between you and her doesn't want you to try and take her hand. Other objects

Figure 47 *Jenny is leaning fairly close to Tom but her legs are swivelled away from him. Her knees are pointing away from him. Tom is, on the other hand, completely turned round to face her.*

which create barriers are umbrellas and briefcases. A variant is keeping one's hands stuffed in the pockets of one's coat. Men who fret about contact often walk with their hands in their pockets. The body language is clear: 'My limbs are not available for contact.'

A touch too much

All over the surface of the skin a variety of touch receptors react to pressure and other sensations. These receptors fire messages to the brain. The rate and pattern of firing 'tells' the brain whether the touch feels good, bad or neutral. Intense erotic touching can sometimes feel almost like pain. That's because, like painful stimuli, intensely pleasurable ones can over-stimulate the touch receptors. It all feels 'too much'.

Our sense of touch develops in the womb. Babies 'know' what is a loving touch, and what hurts. As we grow up, the sense of touch becomes very sensitive. We can tell whether a caress is gentle, erotic, clammy, irritating, or persistent; whether it is an exercise of power, or an expression of love. If I touch you, it can mean either that I feel warm towards you and/or desire you, or that I feel I am dominant. I am touching you because I have the right to touch you. It's an ownership gesture. On a first date, being sensitive about when, and where, you begin to touch is crucial. Men have to be careful not to touch when the woman is sending out neutral or hostile signals. Extraverted men are particularly liable to engage in over-touching.

Tom and Jenny continued . . .

The subjects of our case history are having their problems with touch.

Tom and Jenny know very little about each other's past. There was an awkward moment when he touched her shoulder as he came back with the second round of drinks. But they recovered from her flinching at that and are having a good time in the pub. He wants to ask her back to his flat but he also doesn't want to rush things in case it puts her off.

Tom and Jenny are now sitting on the same side

Figure 48 *This couple may have agreed to have dinner in the hope that romance would be in the air, but the body language at this moment is negative. They are not looking at each other, but leaning away. Eye contact is non-existent since both of them are focussed on their plates. Even their elbows express a hostile attitude.*

51

Figure 49 *This suggests dinner has been going quite well. The couple are beginning to feel able to get close. The woman is smiling and not resisting the invasion of her plate – and space – by the man. Sharing food or tasting the food of your partner is a sign of closeness. If they were feeling hostile her facial expression and position would be quite different.*

of the table. Their body language is instructive. Jenny is sitting turned towards Tom, but while the top half of her body is saying: 'I'm glad to be here with you', the lower half of her body is much more ambivalent (see figure 47).

Tom and Jenny chose one of the most common locations for a first date: a pub. Other favourite activities are going to the movies or going out for a meal.

The restaurant

Sharing food is an old way of creating a bond. It's a popular first date because it gives you a chance to talk and get to know one another. It has its risks, however (see figures 48 and 49).

The cinema

A first date at the cinema is bizarre. For most of the evening, you won't be able to talk to each other. You'll be forced into a very unnatural situation, sitting side by side without any possibility of eye contact.

So why do people do it? Partly because they're shy. Partly because boys sometimes hope to snog in the back of the stalls.

Expert advice: keep your eyes on the screen, keep your hands largely to yourself and make sure you have enough time before and after the show to actually talk to each other.

Holding hands

Tom now cracks a joke which makes Jenny laugh. She changes the position of her legs a little and seems more relaxed. He suggests that as it's a nice summer evening they go for a walk. As they get outside the pub, Tom takes Jenny's hand using the palm-to-palm position (see figure 50).

Palm to palm is the most usual way of holding hands. It needn't signify mad passionate lust. It can be just friendly, if brief. The longer it continues, though, the more intimate it is. In our culture, holding hands is the most frequent first touch.

There are more erotic ways of holding hands: with each finger laced with each other, for example. This is most comfortable when a couple are sitting. The gesture is interestingly ambiguous because it mixes aggression with intimacy. Humans are the only species that can do this.

Holding hands doesn't have to be static. You can use your fingers to stroke and explore your partner's hands. In some ways, these gestures mimic what happens when making love. There are delicate spots on the inside of the wrist and in the soft flesh between fingers. New-age types like to play such games, using excuses like: 'I want to read your love line' or, 'let me see your health line'.

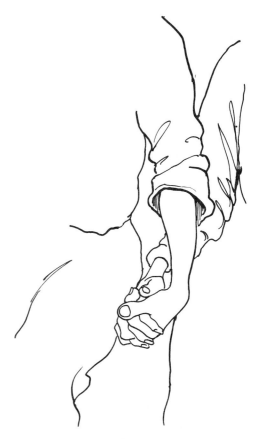

Figure 50 *The palm-to-palm position.*

The first kiss

Tom and Jenny come to a bench overlooking the river and sit down. Tom puts his arm around Jenny's shoulder. He is creating a private space for the two of them. The rest of the world is excluded. She leans her head on his shoulder. Tom has finally got the positive response he wanted.

Figure 51 *Faces ready to kiss.*
The couple are opposite each other. Their lips are slightly parted. They are leaning together. There is also the 'kiss me if you can catch me' pose, where the woman leans back, revealing a great deal of her neck and forcing the man to advance by retreating herself. This mock aggressive 'catch me if you can' is typical chase behaviour which people who are attracted and of equal status engage in. The chase stops being a fun game and becomes an exercise in dominance when, for example, the man puts his hand under the girl's chin and twists her towards him. This use of power is likely to end in trouble or sadness.

Tom now turns towards Jenny and brings his face close to her face. Jenny also turns to him so that their faces are opposite each other. Both their lips are slightly parted.

Songs, poems and literature celebrate first kisses. These celebrations don't often own up to the fact that first kisses are nerve-racking (see figure 51).

In some cultures, erotic kisses don't require you to open your mouth. Eskimos prefer to rub noses, which is considered the height of passion. In some Islamic cultures, kissing is considered not sexy at all, but disgusting. In European cultures, though, serious kissing means opening your mouths and tongue meeting tongue. This kind of kissing crosses the most basic boundary – a boundary into your body. When you hold someone's hand or you let someone put their arm round your shoulder, it's still clear where you end and they begin. Bodies may be touching but they are not merging.

Open-mouth or 'French' kissing is a sort of penetration. You are letting someone across the boundary into your body. Kissing is not generally seen as being as intimate as intercourse, but some people experience it as more so. Our mouth is in our head, which is the central core of where we feel we are. Between the legs is 'down there', really, *less* personal; so, it's not surprising that some people find open-mouthed kissing rather threatening. You are letting someone else into your body, into your self, your identity.

Not all men or women actually enjoy kissing. Introverted women are most likely to feel fraught about kissing, about letting down one of the defences to their body.

Some modern problems

In the past fifty years, advertising has added to our natural insecurities. Advertising warns us that our bodies may be full of defects. As you kiss someone, you are likely, in some corner of your mind, to have the following kinds of anxieties: 'Do I smell right', 'Is there some lingering B.O. which I haven't exterminated with the right deodorant?' 'Are my teeth sufficiently shiny?' 'Will he or she notice what mouthwash I use?' 'Is there something about the taste of my mouth or my tongue that he or she won't like?'

We worry about how sexy we are and the first time we kiss someone we lay many of those anxieties on the line.

For men, there is an additional problem. They usually still have to make the first move, and this carries with it the risk of rejection. Some women see this as yet another form of patriarchal power. I think there is a different reading, which I've explored at some length in my book, *Being a Man*. Nevertheless, it's true that the person who makes the first move does have some power. With it, goes an obligation to watch out for signals that suggest your date does not want you to approach her (see figures 53 and 54).

Tom gets no such negative signals. He doesn't just kiss Jenny but does something she really likes. He puts his arms right round her to create a really intimate space for the two of them. Many men don't do this because they focus so much on erogenous zones.

First kisses can be very different – explosive, ecstatic, exploratory, exciting, embarrassing and, in a world where many think they are meant to display their sexual prowess, an excuse for showing off.

One modern problem is the Show-Off Kisser –

Figure 52 *Kissing on railway platforms. Couples here forget about the rest of the world. They often use coats and blankets to make even more of a tent for themselves.*

Figure 53 *Here the woman has the initiative. She has turned away to get something. The top half of her body doesn't face the man but the bottom half does. Note how he's leaning intently towards her, showing he wants intimacy and ready to kiss. Is she going to comply or not?*

Figure 54 *This has not gone well. The man has put himself slightly higher than the woman to suggest dominance, but she isn't having it. The distance between them is intimate but their lips are firm. The position reflects a great deal of tension – emotional rather than erotic.*

usually an extravert who thinks he or she is competing for an Olympic medal in tongue aerobics. For such people, kissing isn't a way of expressing affection but a chance to do an ice dancing routine in your mouth. By the time they've done a triple loop between your molars you are getting fed up.

Some men and women fret about how well they kiss because they're anxious about the length and flexibility of their tongues. They feel tongue-tied, even if they're not.

Signs of trouble

First dates are about getting to know someone. You may worry that your date is too aggressive or too insistent on sex. Signs of trouble include persistent attempts to touch, constant references to sex and aggressive postures. The woman is starting to fear that the man can't hear her 'No' at all. He's deaf.

If she had heeded the early body language signs she might have avoided these problems – and gone home early.

End-of-first-date behaviour

Tom asks Jenny whether she wants to go home with him. She says: 'Not this time.' He's disappointed, but he doesn't sulk, which pleases Jenny because she likes him. Tom takes Jenny back to her flat. They now engage in very typical End of First Date Behaviour. Tom hasn't quite given up. He gets off his bike, helps Jenny off and then turns to face her. He is taller than her and looks down on her.

Tom asks: 'Shall I come in?'

'No,' says Jenny.

For the first time, she's irritated because she thinks that she had made it clear that she doesn't want, yet, to go any further. Jenny likes Tom, though, and doesn't want the evening to end badly. So she presents a submissive upward look to him.

Tom takes this as a cue for a kiss. He kisses Jenny and imagines that his bravado kissing will make her change her mind. After some deep kissing, he kisses her ear lobe.

This is an unfortunate mistake. Jenny hates being kissed on the ear lobe. It's the place on her body that gives her the kind of feeling-overload I described earlier. She always reacts by shaking.

Tom is at least sensitive enough to realise something is wrong. 'Sorry,' he says.

'I just don't like my ears being kissed. Remember that, eh,' says Jenny, and smiles.

'O.K.'

Jenny's smiles and her telling Tom to remember not to kiss her ears ends the evening on a good note. Obviously, she wants to see him again and to be kissed by him again. Tom smiles, waits till she's on her doorstep and waves.

Fond farewells

The end of a first date is a moment of truth and a moment of power. How romantic is the goodbye going to be? Is either of you going to suggest you do this again? The initiative is not exclusively with men; increasingly, women will suggest a second meeting.

One of the worst outcomes of a first date is when one person wants a second date and the other doesn't. You are bound to feel depressed if you're the rejected party. There's no fix for this, except to arrange a first date with someone else before too long.

Sometimes, of course, first dates don't end on the doorstep. Someone comes back home with

Figure 55 *There can be a mixed message in a farewell. The man here is obviously eager to start a relationship. The woman is hesitant. She looks depressed, eyes down, avoiding eye contact, her body half turned to flee into her house.*

you. There's no reason for a man to assume if that happens it means that the woman wants to sleep with him. In private, a couple can get to know each other rather better than in a pub or the cinema. Some men, if they take a girl home on a first date, behave stupidly, as if they're a sex machine acting out some formula for 'scoring'.

The over-keen nurd turns the lights down low and puts on soft music the moment you are in the door. Then he sits so close on the sofa that the girl is literally squashed. The reason why such a man is ridiculous is that he's paying no attention to what his date wants or feels.

Personal space

If at the end of a first date you go home with someone, don't rush it. It takes time before you both feel comfortable about entering someone else's personal space. A good way of testing how close they want to get is to make small moves. Both of you then have the chance to stop at any point.

Ask yourself if your partner is reciprocating your behaviour (see figure 56).

When you move closer to them do they shift closer to you, do they stay passive or do they actively move away or say they have to go to the loo? If you lean towards them, do they mirror that leaning? If you look at them, do they look back or look away? People like to be surprised by love, but that is not the same thing as being surprised by someone who leaps on you quite unexpectedly.

In our culture, there is a well established pattern to touching. We expect touching to proceed in a routine sequence. We first let a would-be lover into one bit of personal space, get comfortable with that, and then, into an even more personal space. At each point, there's a choice.

Figure 56 *This couple are mirroring and reciprocating each other's behaviour.*

Understanding body language allows you to judge whether or not someone else likes the way – and the extent to which – you are touching them.

Saying No, hearing No

First dates don't always get physical. Many couples will do nothing more than hold hands. Men especially shouldn't expect any date to include some sex.

Sensitive people are good at testing how the other person feels. By instinct, almost like coming up for air, they pause, move perhaps six inches away so that they can see their date's face, and smile. This gives the other person time and space to respond (see figure 57). This is especially important if they aren't echoing your passion. That may not mean they don't like you, but that they are shy. Either way, you need to know.

Pay attention to whether the person you are with looks down, looks away, smiles lopsidedly or engages in displacement activities that suggest they are not happy.

Sexual politics

I have written this chapter as if I expected it always to be men who made the first physical advances to women. There is a great deal of controversy about whether women now feel confident enough to make advances to men. Many things in sexual politics have changed. No man has any excuse for imagining that women secretly want to be raped, for instance. Older women now can date younger men just as older men have always been able to date younger women. In well-established relationships, women certainly do sometimes make the first physical move. But on first dates, the evidence still suggests very strongly that men usually take the initiative.

In societies where we have spent much of the last twenty years studying the power relations between the sexes we ought by now to be mature enough for men not to force themselves on unwilling women. Every woman has a right to say No at any point in a sexual encounter.

For men that means being especially aware of signs of nerves, hesitancy and rejection.

But such openness and attempts at equality also mean that women have to be clear about what *they* want – and ready to say so.

If a first date goes badly, it leaves both parties feeling depressed. If it goes well, it can be a lovely feeling, for you may be at the start of something that will bring a lot of happiness to both of you.

Figure 57 *The inquiring look*

5

Making Love

After a first date, three things may happen. It may feel like a mistake. It may feel wonderful – you're madly in love. Or it may feel good and well worth continuing, though not magical. In our increasingly self-conscious culture people are much slower to fall in love. To fall madly in love feels almost naive.

Eventually, as your relationship develops, there will come a point where making love is a distinct possibility.

Making love is a watershed. Your relationship with that person will never be the same again – whatever happens. You will have 'known' each other, as the Bible says.

Myths of the Swinging Sixties make it seem as if we all hopped from one bed to another without a care in the world. No one was frightened of AIDS or sexually transmitted diseases. We made love – not war – all the time. In fact, even the 1960s were not so free and easy. There has never been a time when sexual relationships have not produced anxiety as well as joy.

Statistics suggest that in Western countries most people will have had more than one sexual partner by the time they are 25. A 1983 study found that 7% of husbands had had more than 20 sexual partners; 22% between 6 and 20; 42% between 2 and 5. Only 29% of husbands had had only one sexual partner. 57% of heterosexual women had had more than one sexual partner; 17% had had more than six. Most of us are neither totally monogamous nor, really, that promiscuous.

You will probably make love to relatively few people in your life. The first time with your partner is likely to arouse a complex mix of emotions – desire, hope, anxiety, a longing for tenderness. Making love is also being out of control, which some people find terrifying and others exhilarating. These complex feelings will betray themselves in body language.

Typical anxieties when you first go to bed with someone centre on what your partner thinks about you and whether your relationship is at the right stage for sex. Different individuals move at a different pace. Common worries are:

- 'Is this happening too fast?'
- 'Does he/she love me or just want me?'
- 'Am I sexy enough?'
- 'What does he/she expect of a sexual partner?'
- 'Have his/her other sexual partners been terrific in bed?'
- 'Will he/she be gentle if it isn't brilliant at once?'

Our culture teaches us to mask such anxieties rather than discuss them, which makes the process more difficult. Nervous people sometimes act brash to cover up.

If you feel excited and anxious, you are unlikely to take a detached view of how someone else is reacting. In many ways, the last thing you want to do when falling in love with someone is to take a detached view. And yet, ironically, you need to step back a little to notice someone else's responses.

Some people – not always men – will expect that a relationship quickly becomes sexual; other people need to feel very secure before they actually sleep with someone. They may have been hurt in the past. Being sensitive to your partner's pace shows you care about them – and are not just 'scoring' – and it helps make a good relationship.

You need to interpret his or her behaviour sensitively – not just to see what you want to see. And this isn't just important at the start of a relationship. However long you've been together you need to read one another's signals and be aware of the reactions between you.

Passion signs

Writers have long tried to identify the signals that reveal passionate love. There are no signs that apply to everyone. People are individuals. But some of the micro-gestures and signals which convey – and betray – strong arousal in an intimate situation have been identified.

Do you find you are often making intense eye contact?

Is there a sense of you moving together?

Compare the two couples in figures 58 and 59. The couple in figure 58 on the sofa show a lot of mirroring. They are keeping pace with each other, creating a joint personal space. But the couple in

Figure 58 *Moving together*

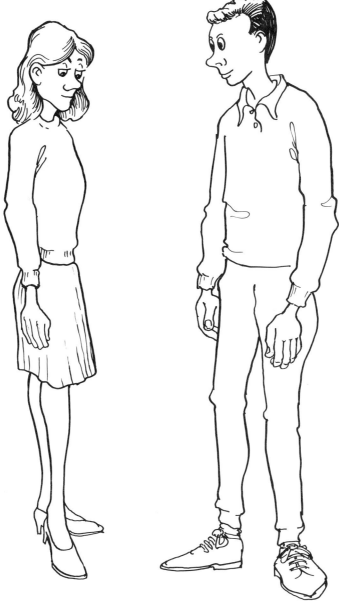

Figure 59 *Problems*

figure 59 are different. The woman has her head down. She is annoyed and evasive.

Alone in a room

Dates usually start in public places. When you are alone together in private, you cross a boundary –

and both partners need to pay attention to the other's body language. The key question is: Is it *giving* or *defensive*?

Someone who feels wary may well choose to sit in a high-backed chair rather than on the sofa. Even if they seem relaxed they will cross their arms and legs – a defensive posture to 'protect' their body.

Staring out of the window is very much a 'playing for time' position. It may reflect nerves. It may reflect second thoughts. The way *not* to deal with the window-starer is to creep up on them from behind, put your hands over their eyes and try to kiss their neck. Much better to stand side-by-side, take their hand and see if you naturally turn to come into a kissing position.

Lying down on a rug by the fire has quite different meanings for a man and a woman. If a *man* does it, it's a very arrogant signal. He's saying, 'I expect you to lie down by me.' If a *woman* does it, it doesn't look so arrogant. Generally, it is still up to men to make the first move. All the woman is doing is suggesting it is appropriate for the man to make a pass at her. But men need to look out here for secondary messages. Some women will combine lying on the rug with a clear Keep-out pose. Keep-out poses include: crossed ankles; hugging a defensive pillow.

Figure 60 *Is this submissive?*

Figure 61
Melting eyes

And what does you own body language tell you about what you are feeling?

Are you touching your body nervously?

If you are a man, do you have the embarrassing feeling that you are about to have an erection?

Personality differences affect the speed at which we interact and our body language style. Extraverts are more impatient, get bored more easily and are more likely to become sexually aroused quickly. They tend to hurry interactions along towards sex. The classic recipe for mismatches of timing are extravert men (going fast) and introvert women (going slow).

There are also intriguing differences in how aggressive and assertive different people – especially men – feel able to be at the start.

The Macho Man tends to put himself in a dominant and aggressive position. He's not concerned about making eye contact or seeing the whole of the woman's face, which suggests he's much less interested in her than in achieving his own gratification. It's all go for his ego.

Figure 62
'Don't look at me like that'

If neither partner is dominant the couple can happily sit side by side on the sofa. They can see all of each other's faces and deliberately explore each other.

The woman in figure 60 has placed herself in a position which is partly submissive but actually allows her to make the first move by touching the man's knee.

Different rhythms of eye contact are likely to accompany each position. The man may make intense and dominant eye contact. He will keep looking at the woman fixedly. He would probably give the same long, highly-aroused looks to a man he was threatening. His sexual partner will respond according to her personality and to how happy she feels. There may well be a conflict. The woman may like the man but hate his style and suspect he's acting macho to cover his insecurity.

In figure 61, the woman returns the eye contact as intensely.

In figure 62 the eye contact is too much, too arousing. The woman tries to avoid it by small head turns away. In animals, looking down tends to be submissive but in humans it's also a sign of avoidance.

Foreplay is forever

The first important thing is to create an atmosphere in which both partners are both comfortable and excited.

What many women say they want is more foreplay. Men need to remember that. Foreplay is play. And a kind of game in which you can use all the body language skills you have.

Foreplay should be fun and a way of exploring what your partner likes. Men forget all too easily that most women like to be touched in places other than the obvious ones. Women often complain that men behave as if they were making love to a head with breasts, genitals and possibly buttocks attached. Worse, the male often acts the rhinoceros – horny but totally without imagination.

Women find this lack of imagination especially irritating because they don't experience their bodies in as divided a way as most men. For men, their erogenous zones are clearly defined. For most women, the boundaries are fuzzier. There are fewer boundaries between the erotic and the non-erotic bits for women than for men.

Figure 63 *'I'm not enjoying this'*

A man can hardly present a questionnaire inquiring where a woman wants to be touched but one can try out touching in different places, gently, playfully, tentatively – and then watch and listen for the reactions.

Many women like the following parts of their bodies to be stroked, caressed, nibbled, felt up or tickled:

- the back of the ear
- the earlobe
- the neck
- the shoulder
- the armpits (it doesn't seem to matter whether the armpit has hair or not)
- the back ('running fingers up and down my spine' is a line in many songs: it shows that songwriters were good sexologists before sexology existed as a profession)
- the inside of the thigh
- the feet (according to the Tibetan *Manual of Tantric Sex*, massaging feet can be very erotic and is an ideal prelude to intercourse; there is no reason to believe Tibetan feet differ from those of other cultures)

Extrovert men need to learn to restrain their impatience while introvert men need to lose their inhibitions. Introverts tend to believe that really there is only one correct way of making love.

As you like it?

The two trickiest problems men face are: timing, and working out if your partner is enjoying what you are doing. Many of the clues are obvious:

Breathing. As sexual arousal increases, the pattern of breathing should get deeper and more relaxed. Breathing patterns change, however, later in love-making. During the 'plateau' phase they tend to

get much shorter and more frantic. During orgasm, the breathing pattern changes quite radically.

Body tone. When you touch any part of your partner's anatomy, do they feel relaxed and give way to it or do they tense up and flinch?

Eyes. Sexual arousal makes the pupils dilate.

Teeth. When highly aroused, women often bare their teeth. This again reflects the close links between sex and aggression. This kind of teeth baring in apes is a sign of extreme aggression.

Men need to recognise signs of anxiety in their partner. Here are some obvious ones:

If people are uncomfortable, they often touch themselves, or hug themselves for safety. Often, too, people fiddle with their fingers, even their ankles, when they feel ill at ease.

The woman in figure 63 is saying: 'You are doing this to me. I'm not protesting but unless you are a moron you can see I'm not enjoying this.'

The woman in figure 64 is sitting up on the sofa and has carefully placed her handbag between her and her partner. She is denying access.

Being alert to these 'No' signals is important. Rushing intimacy makes people angry – and may put them off forever.

Men want: the active-passive bind

If women complain that men are apt to rush and to act as if intercourse were the Everest of sex – conquer it, stay a moment, plant a flag and hurry on down – the main problem for men is that they are still expected to be active and dominant – whatever their personality or the circumstances.

Many feminists argue men don't want women to make the first move, even when a relationship becomes established. It would mean giving up power and control. For many men, the feminist case runs, the ideal woman is passive. Why else do men buy inflatable dolls? Men, they say, are terrified of real women.

Some feminist writers believe heterosexuality *has* to oppress women. Others have tried to suggest ways of improving heterosexual sex; they have argued that no man has the right to expect sex from his partner but also that women should feel they can have the confidence to take the first step. Sex should be an expression of passion – not power.

A key factor is the real freedom to say 'No' –

especially for women.

Many men will enjoy the novelty of a woman they are with making a physical advance. It's not always easy to do, but within the safety and trust of a settled relationship, it should be possible and fun.

The traditional stereotypes of the randy active male and the reluctant passive female are in the process of changing. In fact, women are not always passive (see figure 65).

In one-to-one situations, most women feel less assertive. At a time when both sexes are exploring their roles, women who want a man but feel unable

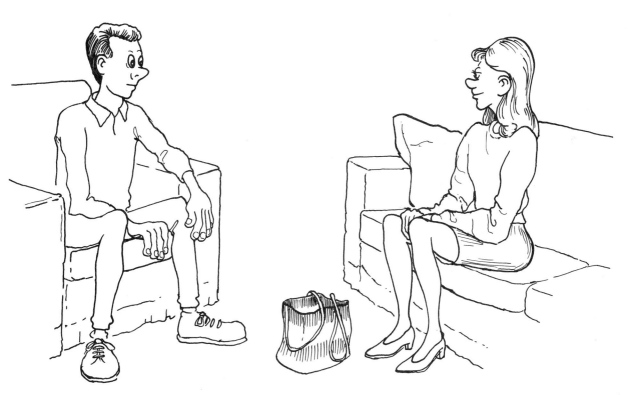

Figure 64 *Barriers*

to do anything about it might start by asking *why* they often feel so powerless to take the initiative.

Is it a question of social convention? 'Nice girls don't do that sort of thing.' Do you somehow cross a boundary and become a 'strumpet', a 'slag' or a 'tart'? Why is it that only sexually-forward *women* attract such derogatory names?

Some women may refuse to be limited by social conventions but may experience feelings that men will find familiar (see figure 66). If they make the first move, will they be rejected? Or perhaps they feel just plain shy. They may even be worried that they don't actually know what to do.

Women who claim to have made passes at men say they have usually had to think about it a great deal, to screw up their courage and to prepare themselves for rejection. Only when they have mapped out in their minds what to do if it goes horribly wrong do they feel able to approach a man.

These convoluted feelings will be revealed in

Figure 65 *Three strong women smiling and laughing together. In groups women laugh, whistle and even cat-call at men. I'm told that in groups they can be very bawdy, too.*

Figure 66 *The shocked male as the woman tries to kiss him. But are men so easily shocked? Will they now think less of a woman who reveals she is highly sexed?*

body language.

A woman who's thinking about making a move will show body language which is balanced between giving positive courtship signals and just the usual receptive ones. She leans forward and takes the man's hand. At the same time, she contradicts these 'active' signals by exuding passive receptive signals. Her legs are slightly parted, her neck is very easy to kiss. The woman is very much in an approach/avoidance tangle of the sort that I describe later.

Some feminists argue that 'come on' stereotypes which are used in male sexual fantasy and pornography don't show women in powerful positions, initiating sex, but in receptive positions. Their body language says that they are oh-so-ready to receive sexual attention but the man still has the privilege of making the first move. Only there is less risk than usual; he is getting strong signals that his advances will be very welcome.

The man in figure 67 is exuding all the courtship signals. The woman is neutral but not hostile. Her knee is pointing out slightly towards him. She is leaning forward a little. Her lips pout, an ambivalent sign that can be sulky or sultry. These are both receptive poses which show she is willing to receive, but the pose is non-committal. He may discover she is happy to be kissed and fondled – or not. She is not giving much away.

Are men frightened of women who do more than signal readiness? Psychoanalysts reported in

Figure 67 *It can be hard to tell what the other is thinking. This is modern man not quite daring to take the initiative.*

the 1950s that some men dreamt of being consumed by giant-toothed vaginas belonging to insatiable women, but there's no evidence men as a whole suffer from such fantasies. Men are much more likely to be frightened of commitment than of 'come-ons'.

These situations give women a choice. They can play the traditional passive role and wait for the man to show he wants them. Or they can go in for a bit of role-reversal and take the lead. That requires self-confidence but it's really not impossible. I want to suggest that if a woman does it sensitively she will be pleasantly surprised both by how good it makes *her* feel, and by how delighted the man in her sights will be.

How to make a pass at a man

It's clearly hardest for a woman to take the initiative at the start of a relationship. After all, if the man wants you, why is he not doing the decent thing and making a pass at you? There may be a whole host of reasons. He may think you are unavailable. He may be unsure whether you would welcome it. He may be nervous. There is the awful possibility that he may not fancy you.

The safest thing to do – and we all like to feel as safe as possible – is to take his hand. This can be a friendship gesture but it most often indicates sexual interest.

Tenderness is a turn on

Sex is loving but also a form of play. It should be tender play. When they face each other both the man and the woman have the chance to play, to see how the other plays and to be tender. They can exchange increasingly intimate smiles, each giving and returning smiles. No one is dominant. Eye contact is mutually intense, well co-ordinated and these looks go with symmetrical smiles. The more you see of each other, the more it allows arousal to build.

Exchanging smiles is a sign of, and a way of increasing, arousal. Often bodies come closer during the smile.

When you are alone in a room, the way you deal with one another's anxieties will reveal a great deal about your social and emotional skills. Sudden movements which you may think are funny and/or erotic but which betray underlying aggressive feelings will only increase anxiety.

Being too aggressive is neither tender nor playful. Sexuality can be a form of power play – something which is not that attractive, especially when most people hope the start of a relationship will be a blend of passion and tenderness.

The approach-avoidance dance

Given that so many taboos, hostility and hopes surround sexuality it's not surprising that people get tense. They can get into a pattern of what is sometimes called *the approach-avoidance dance*. Approach-avoidance expresses the experience of being pulled and pushed in two different directions. We want to do something and so take two steps towards it but we are also scared so we take two steps back. Displacement activities, as described in Chapter 1, and restless moving to and fro, never quite ending up getting close or staying away, are classic examples.

Some couples get stuck in approach-avoidance. Neither person has the confidence to make the first move. The man feels worried he might be rejected. The woman needs greater self-confidence before she can make an advance. Both of you, if you understand that what is happening is typical of approach-avoidance, can help.

For a start, you can easily observe the symptoms in body language which seem to say two different things (see figure 68). Do not do anything sudden. Men should remember that most women hate being 'leaped on'. Come closer bit by bit, seeing how your inching closer is dealt with. Does she retreat or deflect? Does she put up more barriers or welcome your advances?

For women, men who dare not quite take the plunge are a problem. Many women feel it is aggressive for them to take the sexual initiative. One way round this is affectionate touching, which can be imaginative and playful. Some useful ideas include:

- brush his face with a hand
- touch his wrist
- read his palm lines.

Such actions show you feel relaxed and comfortable about touching – and being touched – and you are interested in more.

Personal space

When we make love, we create a new personal space to include the other person. The first time you make love with someone, you are creating personal space together. To succeed, you need to have some sense of the personal space they want and feel happy with.

The trouble is, people have different tastes. Some country lovers like making love for the first time outdoors. But fields can be muddy and there are few such sure-fire passion killers as dropping your yet-to-be-used condom in the mud. For those

73

Figure 68 *Conflicting body language. The woman is leaning close to the man but has one hand near her mouth and another hand on her ankle, so that she is actually coiled to avoid contact while being quite close to him on the sofa. This means: 'I'm interested, but take it slowly, please.'*

who don't have a great affinity with the outdoors, it's safer to make love indoors. Make sure, if you don't have a place of your own, that you will be alone. Nothing creates more tension than worrying about whether you are going to be interrupted.

Moving into the bedroom

A turning point comes when one of you thinks that it might be time to move from the sofa into the bedroom. You then have to stop the flow of foreplay. This is like stopping a dance in mid step: it can wreck your balance.

In an ideal world, you'd both decide simultaneously the moment has come to get into bed. Clothes would melt off in harmony and you'd be wafted onto a cosy silk-sheeted double bed. That's the stuff of fantasies. In most real-life situations, you will be close to falling off the sofa or getting too hot in front of the fire, wondering nervously if the time hasn't come to suggest moving into the bedroom.

Masters and Johnson's theory of the stages of sexual arousal suggests this move can be a problem. You and your partner may not be equally aroused. Worse, the move from the sofa to the bedroom may actually make your partner less aroused.

A good way to make sure you're not going too fast is to ask. Make sure you phrase the question tenderly and in such a way that it's possible for your partner to say 'No', or 'Not now', or 'Not yet'.

Tom and Jenny again

Tom has had previous problems with sex he has not yet felt able to share with Jenny. Some of his partners have found him too aggressive. After a date, Jenny goes back to his flat. They have been drinking and then kissing, and very quickly, he started to feel her breasts. Since she wasn't objecting, Tom assumed she was happy to go further.

'Ready for bed?' he suddenly says.

Jenny had been enjoying the sensation but had only really started to feel excited. His attitude annoyed her. She stood up and asked where the loo was.

'Is something wrong?' Tom asks.

'No,' she snaps.

Tom knows that he has put women off at this stage before. He feels very nervous. When Jenny re-appears, he says: 'That wasn't very romantic. Sorry.'

'You can say that again.'

His apology has mollified Jenny. She lets him take her hand and lead her towards his bedroom. The moment they're in the bedroom, Tom kisses her very passionately again, expecting a passionate response.

Jenny doesn't respond.

'Hold on,' she says, 'Slow down.'

The problem is familiar. Jenny wasn't really ready yet to make love to Tom, especially given the interruption and the mini row. Tom finally listens to what she is saying in words and gestures. Gently, he starts kissing again on the bed. Tom spends a while kissing and cuddling her before the mood returns.

Inhibitions

Tom doesn't know that Jenny has inhibitions about being seen naked. He assumes that now she's enjoying him caressing her breasts, she is ready to make love. She's not. She is making no move towards taking off a stitch of her clothing. She has lit a cigarette and is examining his duvet. This worries Tom since he's nervous about whether he will manage to undo her bra without making a hash of it.

Ironically, Tom's anxiety makes him go more slowly so Jenny becomes very aroused again. It has helped them get over what is often a very difficult moment.

Tom has also spotted some of Jenny's micro-signals, including her attempt to make everything less sexual by paying attention to the duvet design, so he's careful not to rush her.

Naked as nature intended

Human beings have been called 'the naked ape'. But we're an ape that is uncomfortable about being naked. Normally we are dressed. To remove your clothes, to be naked with someone, is intense and tense. Many of us worry about how we look.

Many women worry about the size of their breasts and imagine they are too fat. Many men worry about the size of their chest, the size of their penis and their ability to summon up an erection when they need it. One of the arts of making love is to relax your partner and show that you are enjoying – not silently criticising – their body.

Taking your clothes off shouldn't be done in a terrific hurry. It shouldn't be done in glaring light. Soft light or candles make it easier for people who feel shy because they worry they haven't got the perfect body. It's important not to make your partner feel you're scrutinising them.

Many men and women enjoy being undressed. It's not only erotic. It's curiously comforting because it reminds one of being a child. We're in someone else's hands. The trouble is that clothes are an obstacle course. Many of us are scared that we won't be able to undress our partner stylishly. This isn't surprising. When you try to undress someone of the other sex, you are dealing with unfamiliar clothes that have hooks, zips and buttons in odd places. Love-making should be tender and erotic but it also has its funny side sometimes. The only thing to do is try not to take yourself too seriously!

People are sometimes extremely shy about a particular part of their anatomy. A man may think that his penis is too small. A woman may think her breasts are too small or that her bottom is too large. Introverted women are particularly liable to worry about how sexy they look when naked.

Knowing what your partner wants

Most of us when we make love the first time want to please and impress our partner. It's a way of showing you really care.

There are so many myths about sex and pressure on people to perform that it's easy to think sex has to be more than just tender, emotional and romantic. From the first moment of making love, it has to be mind-bending, orgasmic, a triumph of sexual prowess. In fact, the first time is likely to involve a great deal of trial and error, as you learn what your new partner likes and they learn what you like.

You will find out a lot if you pay attention to how your partner responds. You should literally listen and feel for where your partner likes to be touched.

Listen for their breathing. It is actually much harder to fake the rhythm of breathing than moans of pleasure.

Make sure you don't just touch the obvious spots. Often men touch women too fast and too roughly. They don't continue touching particular parts of the body for long enough. Men often want to move on. But men should learn not to be impatient. Extrovert men need to pay particular attention to that.

Touching spots

Once you are lying together in bed, to some extent you have to start again. You may feel excited, but if you were anywhere near Masters and Johnson's 'plateau' phase you will have come down again to a lower level of arousal.

It takes time to kiss and stroke each other back to high arousal. Many women complain that feminism has had one strange result. Some men are so concerned about bringing women to orgasm that they focus exclusively on the clitoris. This 'magic' spot will make women come. So men pay no attention to stroking other parts of the body. They have forgotten how erotic just holding their partner tight can be and how that can stimulate more arousal.

Stroking

Stroking someone should usually be gentle – especially the first time. Later, when you have been lovers a while, you may actually ask if someone likes to be squeezed more roughly. The first time err on the side of gentleness. You can stroke, kiss or rub, but remember that what you are doing is making love not trying to remove a stain with a dishcloth.

Safer sex

One of the anxieties you are both likely to have is whether it is safe to make love to this person. It's very hard to ask the questions you need to:

1. Where have you been before?
2. With whom? And what do you know about them?

It's a moment of potential embarrassment, and you will both be aware of the microsignals of tension until one of you takes the initiative.

Men have tended to let women worry about contraception. As many women have pointed out, if men had babies, we would have had better contraceptives long ago.

In the 1960s and 70s, when the Pill offered a great breakthrough, men often assumed the woman they were sleeping with was on the Pill. If she wasn't, why didn't she say? For many men, this was an easy way out. Today, with the problem of AIDS, it's just not possible to avoid the subject of contraception and safe sex if you are going to have any kind of responsible sexual relationship.

When AIDS was first discovered it was seen as a homosexual disease. There was nothing for heterosexuals to worry about. Slowly the facts suggested it had been very unwise for so-called 'straights' to be so complacent.

The enormous amount of research done on AIDS has not made it clear how great is the risk for whose who are exclusively heterosexual. Is it mainly confined to those who also inject drugs intravenously? Is it only a real threat in Africa, where the heterosexual population in many countries is very badly affected? How many men have had bisexual phases in their lives which might put them more at risk?

In these circumstances, both partners at the start of a relationship have a responsibility to talk about safe sex and contraception. Sadly, we live at a time when it just isn't safe to assume that anyone isn't HIV positive. The number of sexual partners someone has, or hasn't, had is no guarantee. What's known as 'the tree of sexual contact' shows how you may become infected even though your partner sincerely believes that he or she has never had intercourse with anyone who is at risk.

The main rule of safe sex is to use a condom every time and avoid anal intercourse. The current research indicates fairly clearly that there is a risk of catching the AIDS virus only through blood, semen, anal intercourse or vaginal fluids. You can kiss someone as much as you like on the lips and anywhere else apart from the genital areas.

Many men hate condoms. They are weird to put on and they feel funny. However 'extralite' or 'waferthin' they claim to be, they are a barrier to a key sexual gratification. Nevertheless, they are inevitable at least at the start of a relationship.

If you feel that you are settled with someone and you have worries about previous sexual partners, then it may be worth considering you both taking an HIV test because you will then know, within a committed relationship, that you don't need to use condoms. But do take good advice about this, because the test doesn't show infection until the virus has been in the blood-stream for three months, so it's not an instant precaution.

From the point of view of contraception, too, condoms have many advantages. They have no side effects; they work if you use them. The Pill, the diaphragm and the IUD can all cause women problems.

What AIDS has done is to remind people of the value of non-penetrative sex, which can be fun and obliges lovers to be much more imaginative than they might otherwise be. It's very important for couples to talk about contraception and condoms. After all, if you're close enough to go to bed you're close enough to discuss these things.

The important thing

The key thing about the first time is not to feel under too much pressure. The first time you make love with someone is not the time to prove that you are a sexual athlete. What is important is to feel relaxed, warm, sensual and to give your new partner the feeling that you aren't expecting Olympic-medal sex. Don't worry about whether you have an orgasm or your partner has an orgasm. It's nice if it happens but it shouldn't be ranked as disaster if it doesn't.

The concept of *good-enough love-making* owes something to the psychoanalyst D. W. Winnicott. Winnicott devised the idea of 'good-enough parenting'. Many of his patients were driving themselves neurotic by worrying about whether they were being perfect parents. Winnicott argued that to make children feel warm, secure and listened to might not be perfect but it was a good enough. We need a similar sense of humility about making love. You won't always achieve fantastic mutual orgasms, but you shouldn't think your love-making is a failure because of that.

Body language gives us an ideal way of telling a person you have those warm feelings. When you're making love, kiss them and continue stroking them. Don't just focus on the genital mechanics. It's actually permitted to smile, talk and snuggle with someone in the middle of intercourse!

It's also very sensible to be on the watch for any sign that your partner doesn't like what you are doing. If they flinch or feel ticklish or just lie inert while you do something, stop doing it. And ask.

Don't expect to get everything right the first time round. The concept of good-enough love-making allows you to be less than a totally perfect sex machine.

How was it for us?

Many things can go wrong the first time you make love. You may have a horrible surprise. The man you thought was Mr Right may turn out to be far more aggressive than you imagined.

Some kinds of love making are very off-putting. But the fact that the earth didn't move shouldn't put you off if you are really fond of each other. With time, things should get better.

One of the pleasures of a permanent relationship is that it allows you to build up trust and trust makes sex easier. A trusting and tender relationship should allow you to say what you really like – and to discover things about your sexuality that you didn't know before. But these things are not easy to say, which is why both men and women need to be very attentive to intimate body language.

Developing a relationship is probably more complicated now than ever before. Tradition claims women are the more romantic sex: 'The sweet things are always falling in love.' Once upon a time, perhaps, but many modern women are wary of men. Many men seem to be poor at emotional communication and unwilling to commit themselves. Many women are more likely to test men and to make demands than ever before – practical demands. Women's magazines constantly tell women that one of the rewards of feminism is that they have a right to good sex too. Wham Bam, Thank You, Mam might have worked once (though I doubt it) but it certainly won't do for Ms 2000!

Intimate body language

When you are in bed with someone, you are very close to them, but you can't rely on many of the cues you normally use. You are too near to them. Most social interactions in our culture take place at a distance of between 3 feet and 7 feet. A situation has to be very emotional for two people to come closer than 3 feet.

Ironically, the closer you get to each other, the more personal space you share and the less you actually see of your partner. Many of us make love 'blind'. Many people close their eyes when they kiss and during intercourse. Women are more likely to do this than men. When asked why, people say it feels romantic and allows them to concentrate on the feelings of touch. But the consequences are curious. With our eyes shut, we blot out a great deal of information about the world and our partners.

At first this may not matter because everything feels so heady but over time it will. The average couple makes love over 5 times a week when they first start having a sexual relationship. That figure declines with time. According to a recent study, over 40% of married people say they make love an average of 3 times a month after 7 years.

Sex is not the be all and end all of any relationship but it is an important cement that bonds people. It makes a caring relationship all the more exciting.

Touching feelings

As we see less than usual in bed, we need to rely on other senses to know how the other person is feeling. But our sense of touch is curiously less practised. Experiments show that people are not very skilled at identifying objects by touch alone or at explaining what they enjoy physically. That's why it's very important to check out what your partner wants.

Women want

Women often complain that once men get used to having a relationship they tend to presume sex will be on tap. They ignore the nice preambles – flirting over a drink, saying how sexy their partner looks and engaging in playful touching that is arousing. Getting someone in the mood is an important skill if you are going to keep a relationship exciting. Men need to learn to rate themselves as lovers not just in terms of sexual prowess.

Figure 69 shows a woman who is purring with pleasure. She is in no hurry to move on. She thinks that having her back rubbed while she reads *Cosmo* is a perfect delight.

When a woman takes the initiative she may want to half-arouse, half-tickle her lover by exploring those bits that aren't the obvious erogenous zones. She strokes the hair on his arms, his belly button, between his toes. All sweet, sexy games that delay actual sex.

The personal is the political

Within a caring, settled relationship, most people feel freer to explore their sexuality – to find out what they want. Feminism and sexual research have also had a very clear influence on how people make love. The most interesting change is that women have become much more assertive about getting their sexual needs met. Women are less willing to put up with sexual frustration. Alert men need to be aware of micro-signals which reveal frustration – especially after they have made love. The kind of signals I mean are:

- irritability, and moving out of touching range
- doing something else quickly
- touching herself constantly.

This book is not a sex manual or a suburban Kama Sutra, or a Guide to Position 33B ('How to make love on the trapeze while eating your partner's orange'). But our greater awareness and openness about sex makes it possible to examine the advantages of some love-making positions.

The 'missionary position' is said to have got its name during the time of the British Empire: African women giggled that the clergymen who came to convert them only made love with the man on top. The man is dominant and controls the rhythm of love-making. It allows both partners to look directly at one another. Intense eye contact is easier in this position than in any other. It's quite hard though for the man to use his arms to stroke or caress his lover since he needs them to balance. It's also virtually impossible for either partner to see the pubic triangle so the position

Figure 69 *No hurry to move on*

actually cuts out a strong source of visual stimulation. In this position women sometimes feel not that they are making love *with* their partner, but that love is being made *to* them.

Microsignals to look for:

• a kind of passivity
• fairly even breathing, which suggests there was no climax.

'Girls on top' became a popular position largely as a result of the unlikely combination of the research of Masters and Johnson and feminism. The body language is interesting, because the woman is in the dominant position. She controls the rhythm of love-making by straddling the man. Interestingly, it's a position which makes eye contact harder. Men are sometimes puzzled by the fact that women keep their eyes open in this position – a sign that they are more in control – but they don't look at the man below. Rather, women tend to look into the middle distance.

There are, of course, dozens of different (and perfectly comfortable) positions. In a settled relationship, you should be able to discuss which you both like, as trust develops. For men, the crucial thing is not to become complacent and unromantic. Compare sex and food. Most times you share a meal with a partner you will spend 30 to 60 minutes sitting down, talking and eating. If you go out to a restaurant, you will probably spend much longer. Why rush sex more? Flirting with your partner, getting ready to go to bed, foreplay, making love and snuggling and talking afterwards deserve to have time set aside. One of the pleasures of a settled relationship is spending Saturday or Sunday morning in bed. Even if you have children, you can manage to do this once they are old enough to amuse themselves for a while by watching TV.

Orgasm

We live in a very self-conscious and sex-conscious society. We increasingly feel it's vital to get everything we can out of a relationship. In a settled relationship, both partners will want to have orgasms. For men this is usually not a problem. But for women it can be.

There are two kinds of female orgasm – vaginal orgasm and clitoral orgasm. One woman has described the complexity of feelings during orgasm nicely: 'Suddenly after the tension built and built I was soaring in the sky, going up up up. My insides were tingling. My skin was cool. My heart was racing in a good way and it wasn't easy to breathe.' Another described it as feeling like a cork popping out of a bottle of champagne.

Feedback and faking

Men often worry that women fake orgasms. Some feminist writers have claimed that many women felt it was part of their role to make their men feel like great lovers. The film *When Harry Met Sally* had a scene in a restaurant where Sally brought everything to a stop by demonstrating to Harry how she faked an orgasm. All it required was the ability to moan, groan and shake with lots of energy. Men, Sally suggested, needed to hear such noises to satisfy their egos. The scene was so much discussed, partly because men have come to worry that women are 'faking it'. Many men have become obsessed with how good their performance is.

Such concern is new. In the past most men weren't that interested in what women really experienced.

In a good relationship, couples give each other verbal and non-verbal feedback. If the woman you have just been making love with is caressing you gently and trying to tickle you, you probably needn't get too neurotic about the size of your penis or how many multiple orgasms she's had. What is important is for men to give women feedback too, physically and verbally. The relationship is more likely to grow if both of you remember to say how good it is when it is good. It's sad how easily both men and women can become careless about that.

The tender touch

One useful thing to remember is that touching in a relationship need not just be about sex. There are lots of gentle, positive ways of showing affection which don't have to be preludes to another mega-orgasmic tumble.

Most women will be nicely surprised if their lover sometimes holds them or cuddles them or strokes them when sex is not in the offing. These are parts of body language we tend to ignore. I suggest readers think about the following questions:

- How often do you touch your lover when making love is not in your mind?
- Where do you touch them affectionately?
- How often do you just hug them?
- Do you kiss them when kissing is not a prelude to sex?
- For how long?
- Many couples spend many evenings watching television. Do you sit next to each other when you do so?

There is more to a good sexual relationship than mere sex. Understanding the intricacies of body language should make you much freer about this kind of touching which doesn't have an end in view.

Figure 70 *Snuggling up*

Après sex

One of the perennial complaints women have about men is that after they make love, they want to get on with the next thing or they fall asleep. Men need to be sure to pay attention to the afterglow and continue to stroke their partner and to snuggle up.

Making love should be a mixture of affection and excitement. A good lover acts and reacts. He or she watches what the other person's body is doing and enjoying. For men, the challenge (and the fun) is partly to lose control (which is not easy to do because we are such a controlling sex) and to manage that while really paying attention to your partner's feelings. For women, the challenge is to have the confidence to ask for what you want and to have the generosity not always to be the passive one. If you manage that, the chance is that you'll be making love to the same person for a long time.

6

Everyday Touching,
Everyday Tensions

Chapter 5 concentrated on sex. Few relationships survive on sex alone, however. We expect to do more with our lovers than make love. Not many books, however, offer advice on the more prosaic aspects of relationships. How to shop together, how to spend evenings out or how to garden together is not the stuff of bestsellers. Yet most couples will spend far more time in those non-erotic pastimes than in bed.

One intrepid psychologist timed his behaviour over nine months (see figure 71). He found that he spent far more time drinking – often very happily with his wife and friends at their local pub – than doing anything very intimate. His experiences emphasise an interesting paradox. Relationships depend on a couple enjoying many unerotic activities together – shopping, parenting, going out, having compatible friends, being able to agree on what wallpaper to hang.

Sex is extremely important. If one partner feels constantly frustrated, it will affect everything else. But while bad sex can destroy a relationship, good sex by itself won't make it succeed for very long.

This paradox makes it important to look at body language out of bed as much as in bed.

Everyone has individual ways of reacting to stress and showing distress – personal SOS signals. When things go badly, it's often hard to speak

Figure 71 *A time graph showing the relative amounts of time spent in various activities*

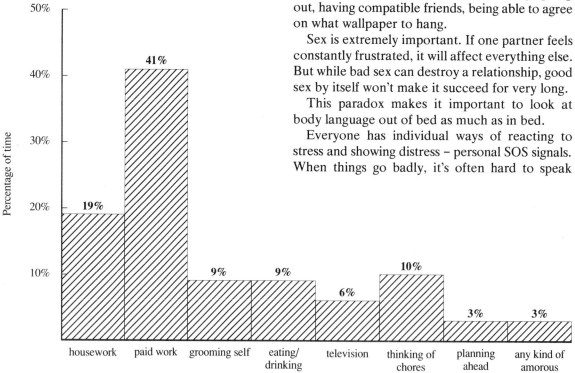

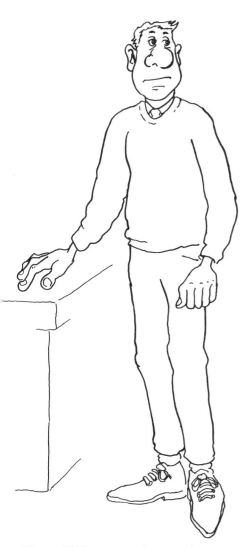

Figure 72 *Suppressed aggression*

about it, so one mark of a good relationship is the ability of each partner to read the other's SOS signals early on and so prevent crises.

One of the things that creates tension around everyday activities is our different expectations.

The joy of shopping

The saying is: 'This woman was born to shop'. I've never heard that said of a man. Many men's feelings about shopping echo those of Victorian ladies about sex. You close your eyes, think of Britain (or, at least, the British economy) and hope it doesn't last too long. A TV ad for McDonalds illustrates male antipathy to clothes shopping. A young man is slowly driven berserk as his girlfriend wanders from shop to shop. She can't decide which outfit looks best so the whole day is frittered away in what he thinks is silly agonizing.

Failure to observe body language in such situations may lead to an explosion.

In figure 72, the woman has tried on twelve dresses. The man thinks she looks fine in ten of them. He is trying to conceal how bored he is. He is standing by a counter and is trying hard not to drum his fingers. His fingers are under control, but his mouth is asymmetrical, his eyebrows arched and his eyes are looking into the middle distance. By the time she shows off Outfit 13 he has almost reached breaking point. He has put his clasped hands behind his back, and is twisting the fingers of one hand round the thumb of the other – a sign of suppressed aggression.

In order to get him out of this mood, the woman has to do rather more than smile and ask how he thinks she looks. But she is in a somewhat narcissistic state. In fact, his lack of enthusiastic response makes her feel unappreciated.

Other forms of displacement activity men engage in while women shop reveal a mixture of boredom and a not-too-unconscious wish to run away. Common displacement activities include the slumped sit and minute examination of shoes, the eye pinch and the meditative analysis of the contents of one's wallet.

Men are usually highly susceptible to the sight of attractive women but the one place they are unlikely to ogle is in a boutique. An alternative male pose is sitting with one's hands underneath one's bottom (see figure 73). This is an attempt to comfort oneself while being ready to spring up and leave.

The relaxed-looking man in figure 74 is, alas, a fantasy, though he does offer a solution to the shopping mismatch. He has brought along a book and a hip flask to pass the time. He and his partner have agreed two rules about shopping. First, he is allowed to read as long as he looks up and pays attention to her when she is trying out a new outfit. That way she gets the critical attention

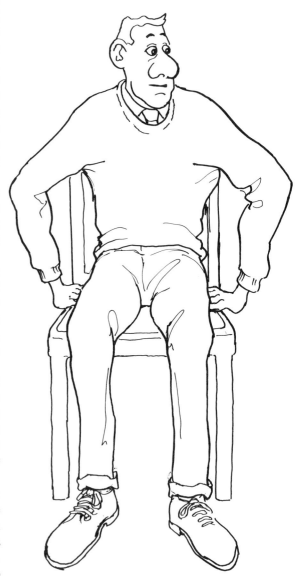

Figure 73 *The slump*

Figure 74 *The enlightened shopper*

she wants from her partner but he need not get demented while she is changing or deciding what next to try on. Second, they take a coffee break every 90 minutes.

Supermarkets

Supermarkets don't have the effect on most men that clothes shops do. Going round the super-market together is one of those routines that appears to sustain a relationship. When food shopping, however, the man is quite as likely to exasperate the woman as vice versa. Men often get obsessed with finding bargains. They think the weekly shop is a chance to show how good they are at cost-efficiency analysis.

Body language at the supermarket is revealing from the moment you pick up the trolley. She or he who controls the trolley becomes the leader of this operation. The person without the trolley usually follows slightly behind (the low-status position). Observers of supermarket behaviour have often noted trolley wars as one partner tries to regain control of the trolley.

Does it sound childish? Absolutely. But one of the joys of relationships is that they allow us to regress to the level of two-year-olds, squawking 'It's mine', 'No, it's *mine*'.

In figure 75, the woman had been pushing the trolley. But the moment she stopped to buy pasta, the man grabbed it and wheeled it to the delicatessen counter. She looks exasperated as she sees 'her' trolley disappear.

Mature couples swop control of the trolley during buying so that no one is in total control. But such collaboration doesn't come easily.

Shopping often seems to bring out those personality traits we find most annoying in our partners. Many couples now shop after they have finished the day's work, when both are trying to shed the stress of the day. That can aggravate any tensions between them.

The intensely preoccupied man in figure 76 is driving his partner berserk. He is comparing the price of various brands of soap powder. He is wondering whether the Own Brand is as good value as the Named Brand. His face betrays total

Figure 75 *Trolley wars*

concentration on a comparison of prices, weights and ingredients. His partner has already sniped that maybe next week he'd like to bring his calculator along. She doesn't like this superior attitude of his, which comes out in other parts of their lives, too. She is trying to work out what both their children will eat over the next week. Doreen is twelve and is determined to lose weight; Harry plays sports and can eat like a horse. *She* doesn't want to cook a different meal for everyone, an issue *he* blithely ignores, since he doesn't do the cooking.

Figure 76 *Which brand?*

By the check-out point, hostility rages. She is letting him unload the trolley on his own. Meanwhile, she has gone to get some last-minute items. He is terrified that she won't come back in time to pay. She has the cheque book. He frets that the check-out girl will demand payment and he'll have to wait and look stupid till she turns up.

The man in figure 77 has lost his partner in the supermarket. Not knowing where she is makes him highly stressed. It's reflected in the way he has piled all the groceries into his trolley in an over-controlled way. He can impose his will on packets even if he can't on his partner.

The Competitive Couple shop together but argue constantly over what to buy. They face each other across the trolley. Each picks up, almost as a trophy, the item they want and brandishes it at the other.

At the check-out

Shopping conflicts have the potential to develop into major episodes of tension and of silence. People express their displeasure with each other in the way that they unload their trolleys and in the positions that they take up at the check-out.

One of the curious aspects of social life is the privacy that surrounds money. You don't peek when your partner taps in his number into the cashcard machine. So at the till the man doesn't watch while the woman writes the cheque but piles things into carrier bags.

This couple may not need marriage guidance but they need shopping guidance. Their little war with each other is spiralling out of control. From the moment when he annoyed her by comparing brand prices, they have been upping the ante. You could write it in blank verse:

Figure 77 *Lost soul*

Figure 78 *Creating barriers in the car*

You are irritating me.
The more you irritate me,
the more likely I am
to irritate you.
I know that,
when irritated,
you do your best
to irritate me.
I expect the irritating worst.

Is there any solution to this? Before you sleep with someone, should you go shopping with them first? Signs of stress, like gripping the trolley too hard or aggressively striding straight to the items they want, should be noted. Unless things are going very badly, you can deflect the irritation spiral by doing something simple, like touching your partner's neck – a form of nice grooming behaviour which establishes contact.

There are some couples who manage to shop in a highly collaborative way and to enjoy doing it. They really share the trolley. They show each other what they would like to buy if it's something out of the ordinary. They choose things that they know the other person will like. At the check-out, you see them unloading the trolley together and then both packing together.

Sulking in cars

Few books have been written about what is an important modern phenomenon – interpersonal crises in cars. People prefer to dream of cars as erotic. Oh, the smell of the leather of the back seat! In all likelihood, however, there's more sulking than sex in cars. Cars are small. You are close together. But human beings are inventive. We can use enforced closeness to create miles of interpersonal distance. You may be inches apart and a universe away.

In figure 78, the driver has adjusted the mirror. His message is: 'I can't be bothered to think of you.' The couple are looking in different directions. Without setting out to do it, the woman has slid well away from the man and out of touching range. Her toes are pointing away from him. She uses her hand to wipe off some dirt from the window, very much a displacement activity. Her other hand hovers near the handle for the window. She is ready to get out.

Figure 79
*The 'let's compromise'
head shake*

Signs of stress in cars include drumming on the steering wheel and gripping it too tight. Some men like to show off and hardly grip the wheel at all.

The fact that people are close together in a car does make it possible to devise strategies for coping with tensions. If you notice that your partner is tense, you can first shift your body so that you are turned towards them, not away from them. The 45-degree turn is not confrontational.

It's very important not to confuse the Let's Compromise head shake (see figure 79) with a negative head shake: the Let's Compromise usually also involves a slight shoulder shrug.

Having a good trip

One of the pleasures of really being together is that you share secrets from the outside world. Your very intimacy is a secret. You can sometimes see this in couples who are travelling together on trains. To the unskilled observer, they look quite

92

cool but, in fact, everything about their body language reveals how close and sexy towards each other they feel.

The couple in figure 80 might look as if they are disenchanted with each other. Each of them is reading the paper. Neither is looking at each other, but their body language reveals that they are intensely and comfortably aware of each other's bodies and of what each other is thinking. She is taking a peek at what he is reading; he has nudged his shoulder close to her shoulder. Their thighs are touching, too.

Eating people is sexy

There was a famous scene in the film *Tom Jones* in which the hero and a lady gnawed their way

Figure 80 *Companionable silence*

through dinner as a prelude to gobbling each other up in bed. Recently, and less dramatically, I was walking down the street when I saw a couple enact a love scene with bread sticks. They weren't doing anything remarkable or obscene. They were walking absolutely level with each other. They were both eating bread sticks. Their faces were turned towards each other as they munched. The woman leaned lightly back exposing her neck and smiling as she ate.

Food has been called a great aphrodisiac. Do you enjoy the way your lover eats? Or does his stuffing himself make you wonder why you are so interested in a man who would have fitted better into a Stone Age milieu where he could gnaw on buffalo bones? Personality differences show both in what we eat and in how we eat. Extraverts tend to eat quickly, messily and are more willing to try new foods. Introverts are fussier and more fastidious.

Very often, when we feel tense, we use food to comfort ourselves. We eat a great deal and talk very little. Some evidence suggests that women in particular use food as a comforter.

Adults often criticise children for their table manners. Adults can't do this to each other (unless someone is doing something amazingly gross), but you will often see people eating together exchanging snide looks of judgment.

Bathroom behaviour

There was a time when feelings of shame associated with the body made certain kinds of activity very private. During the 'three-day week' in 1973, however, when electricity wasn't available for part of the day, the government suggested that couples share baths. The idea was seen as a bit weird, and yet it slowly became clear that more

couples do this than one might think.

It's not surprising couples feel shy about being together in the bathroom. You use the bathroom to wash, floss your teeth and excrete. None seem to be particularly attractive activities. Yet water is relaxing and can be erotic. Young parents often find that the bathroom is one of the few places where they can snatch any privacy during the day.

The surprising revelation is that it is not just young and adventurous lovers who bathe together. John Mortimer wrote a Rumpole story which turned on the bathing habits of a judge and his wife. The judge expressed sympathy with a thief because when he took baths with his wife he was always consigned to the tap end: the poor man couldn't relax because the tap was always digging into his back. The judge identified with his suffering, for his own wife always made *him* take the tap end, and gave him a light sentence. Being condemned to unrelaxing baths, the judge explained, had made the man turn to crime.

In the story it was left to the reader's imagination to guess if either couple bathed together to make love. It's not easy to make love in a bath tub unless it happens to be very large, but that is not to say a bath can't be an excellent place for affectionate foreplay. You can bathe together, with one person leaning back against the other. This is also a good position in which your partner can wash your hair – a nice form of contact.

Showers are better for more energetic erotic activity. You can soap each other all over – a very good way of developing arousal.

Children and other creatures

I have so far written as if relationships occur in a space where the adults are the only beings involved. Real life is messier. A friend of mine

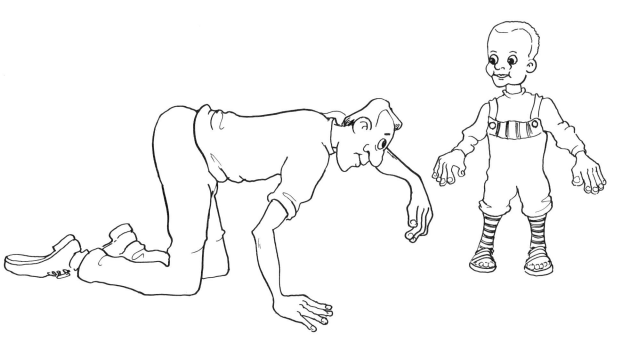

Figure 81 *Playing elephants. The man scampers on all fours and makes funny facial expressions.*

once had a relationship with a woman who had four cats and a parrot who was caged in the living-room. The parrot screeched every morning.

The presence of children changes body language drastically. We are allowed to regress with our own children. A mature man may find himself crawling on all fours, making funny noises and pretending his arm is the trunk of an elephant (see figure 81). The child he is playing with is giggling. But the man's display also affects the woman. She doesn't normally see him being so relaxed. Usually he is Mr Executive, the man with the briefcase. She is very touched by his ability to shed all those inhibitions when playing with their child.

Adults teach children many of the elements of body language by playing with them. They do this partly by using exaggeration and parody. From the age of eighteen months onwards toddlers learn to tell the difference between what is 'real' and what is 'pretend'. Key clues that tell children which is which are the adult's exaggerated facial expressions and gestures.

A common pattern when playing is for adults to first stimulate children and then, after a burst of laughter, to be very comforting and tender. Good parents know children need to be touched.

Current concerns about child abuse have unfortunately made some parents – and especially step-parents – very worried about their children being touched. Children *need* to be cuddled and held. Children deprived of touches, hugs and kisses are much more likely to develop all kinds of behaviour difficulties. A parent should only worry if they see that their partner is concentrating too much on touching one child, or if something furtive seems to be going on. I have made two films about child abuse. There is no doubt that it does happen and, sometimes, it happens in families

Figure 83 *'Leave me alone'*

Figure 82 *A nice, totally appropriate hug for a child. Note the slightly self-conscious smile, though. We worry whether expressing affection like this is OK.*

where you would least expect it. But awareness of the problem of child abuse should not make us so paranoid that we can't touch our children appropriately (see figure 82).

For both your sakes

Most books on body language offer advice on how to use it competitively. The idea is that if you know what someone is *really* thinking, you have an advantage over them. Love is a different kind of trade. You either both win or both lose. One situation in which you are both likely to lose is when things are going wrong, and no one will discuss it. Stress mounts. No one confronts the issues. The signs are clear, and yet everyone avoids dealing with them.

Every individual will show some signs of tension. Some personality types will hide them less than others. Introverts will be ashamed if things are going wrong and will tend to blame themselves. Extraverts will tend to blame the other person.

Anger and after

One of the most worrying things to discover is that your partner is angry, but won't say *why* he or she feels that way. We often can't help showing how angry we are by our gestures and most of us know that an effective way to punish someone is to be angry and refuse to tell them why.

Personality differences matter here, too. Extraverts feel more able to let out their anger. Introverts are more likely to bottle it up, though when it is finally released it is liable to erupt in vitriolic ways.

The easiest signs of anger to detect are 'keep away' signs.

When your partner displays a 'keep away, leave

Figure 84 *The lip tremor. A clear sign of anger being repressed.*

Figure 85 *The person lying in this bed is sharing a bed with a stranger, not sleeping with a partner. They have each made a nest on their side of the bed.*

me alone' signal (see figure 83), an unaggressive approach after a few minutes may well succeed in getting one's partner to reveal what's up.

Introverts are much more likely than extroverts to withdraw when they get angry. They may even appear to be acting normally. Tell-tale signs of stress to look out for include changes in tone of voice (they might be a little clipped), and an increase in slight involuntary movements (see figure 84).

We often express our psychological problems physically – in tension, tiredness or indigestion. Human beings inevitably play both happy and sad games with each other. When a relationship is going wrong, people who like to be in control will tend to play games far more than before.

A common destructive game is 'I'm not going to bed at the same time as you'. There are two ways of doing this. The hostile partner will either insist on going to bed early, or on staying up late. Either way, they are denying you both the comforting contact which may bring you back into communication.

A couple's life is getting badly 'out of sync' when this happens. If they want to make up they need to do something quickly, or the next step will be that someone will decamp out of the bedroom. For some people, insisting that you talk about what's wrong may be the best answer. For others, non-threatening, non-sexual touching can be a way of re-opening communication (see figure 86). Men should be especially careful to let their partner (who is probably in a mood to misunderstand) know that they want to sort things out, not just to have sex.

It is no fun being in a relationship when things are going wrong. Sometimes, however, the signs of stress become even more acute.

Figure 86 *Non-threatening touch*

Breaking down, breaking up and rejection

Is your partner having problems sleeping? Waking early is often a symptom of depression. What do they do if they wake early, toss and turn or get up? Tossing and turning need not be the sign of some deep-rooted crisis, but if your partner isn't sleeping well, you should ask why. If they start talking about their dreams, listen, but don't rush in to interpret. Let them say first what they think.

Most relationships break up because of violence, infidelity or drink. Many people say they always know when the other person is being unfaithful. They become erratic; their love-making changes. I suspect that when people do worry something is wrong, it's more often due to sensing a sudden kind of distance, and to putting simple clues together. When a man's job suddenly involves many trips out of town or late nights at the office, for example, he may well be up to something.

The only way that understanding body language can help is that it may allow you at a relatively early stage to put out 'compromise' signals. These make it clear to your partner that you're not just saying you want to sort out your difficulties, but that you really are sincere about it. The trouble is, there may be too much anger for you to be able to give out such non-confrontational signals.

In many ways, the body language of a couple when they're dealing with these problems mimics the high arousal of their early dates. But this time the arousal is due to anger and fear rather than desire.

We're all afraid of losing relationships. One marriage in three breaks up. People still hope this relationship will be forever but know it may not happen. Understanding body language should, at least, make you see the warning signals early on. This gives you a chance to try and mend things and, if that fails, it will stop you being surprised if there is a break-up.

7

How Well Did You Score?

The questions I put in 'Where you start from' (see pages 13–14) reveal the kind of attention you pay to body language.

1. The more aware of other's gestures, the more attentive you are to body language. Obvious enough.

2. Did you list 5 things pretty much off the top of your head or did you have to think about it? The more you have to think, the less instinctively aware of body language you are.

3. The same goes as for 2.

4. The quicker you made your lists for 2 and 3, the more you've integrated awareness of body language into your everyday perceptions.

5. The more time you spend looking at other people's faces, the more aware of body language you are.

6. One of the skills that people who are good at body language have is that of making up scripts about other people, imagining their lives.

7 & 8. Were these easy to do or do you have to struggle? The more the struggle, the more you need to have read this book.

9. A trick question. Only the obsessive notice *only* the body language. Chat-up lines also matter!

10. If you are always surprised that is bad news.

It's worth comparing how you did initially with these questions with how you do after you've read this book – and decided to pay attention to body language!

I hope that by now you understand a good deal about the *theory* of body language. You need, however, to practise and sharpen your awareness of it in real life.

We all need love and are frightened of not getting enough. If we have it, we are frightened of losing it. Understanding your partner's body language doesn't spare you making embarrassing mistakes either when you start a relationship or later on, but it should make the experience richer and more fun. Greater knowledge won't guarantee happiness or that you're never taken by surprise, but you will know a great deal more of what is going on around you – whether or not people tell you what they feel.

The lyrics of a famous song include the wise line: 'The love you take is equal to the love you make'. The Beatles were singing something quite profound – something that we can use to make the most of our lives.